The Washington Post
DESKBOOK ON STYLE

The Washington Post
DESKBOOK ON STYLE

Compiled and Edited by
ROBERT A. WEBB

MC GRAW-HILL BOOK COMPANY

New York • St. Louis • San Francisco • Düsseldorf
London • Mexico • Sydney • Toronto

Book design by Judith Michael.

8 9 10 11   BKP BKP   8 9 8

Library of Congress Cataloging in Publication Data
Main entry under title:

The Washington Post deskbook on style.

   Bibliography: p.
   Includes index.
   1. Journalism—Handbooks, manuals, etc.
I. Webb, Robert A.
PN4783.W35   651.7'402   77-22958

ISBN 0-07-068398-0 pbk.

CONTENTS

ACKNOWLEDGMENTS

The preparation of this manual would not have been possible without contributions from many of my past and present colleagues on the staff of The Washington Post. I am especially grateful for research material provided by Fred Barbash, Jack Eisen, Mark Hannan, William MacKaye, Susan Morrison, Sunday Orme, Valarie Thomas and Tom Wilkinson; for detailed suggestions by Robert Ames Alden, James Clayton, George Lardner Jr., Peter Masley, John MacKenzie, Mason McAllister, Robert Payne, Ralph Reikowsky, Jay Ross and William Smart; and for the support of The Post's senior editors—Benjamin Bradlee, Howard Simons, Richard Harwood and John Lemmon.

My thanks also to Donna Crouch and Pamela Whitehead for typing the several drafts and to Cheri Eddy for typing the final manuscript.

James O'Connor, of Silver Spring, Md., read much of the manuscript and made many valuable suggestions in the hope of saving the English language from journalistic abuse.

Anonymous journalists from coast to coast also contributed to this book, for—although most material in it is original—some rules and examples were suggested by a reading of the stylebooks of a dozen other newspapers. They are The Baltimore Sunpapers, The Chicago Daily News, The Chicago Tribune, The Detroit Free Press, The Detroit News, The Los Angeles Times, The Miami Herald, The New York Times, The St. Louis Post Dispatch, The St. Petersburg Times and The Washington Star.

R. A. W.

HOWARD SIMONS
PREFACE

At best, a newspaper catches history on the run.

A newspaper never is complete or completely accurate. Some of the reporting, writing and editing is exemplary. Some is ho-hum. A newspaper is uneven from day to day, and uneven from page to page on any given day. The Washington Post is no exception.

What a newspaper often lacks is consistency—a style, if you will. One way for a newspaper to establish consistency without detracting from the personal styles of its writers is to set forth a body of rules. These become the elements of style, as the master stylist William Strunk Jr. and his student E. B. White called them.

Other newspapers have different rules, different audiences, different resources, different needs. But to the extent that common sense informs this stylebook, it can be useful to all.

This, then, is what our stylebook is about. It attempts to provide the reporters and editors of The Washington Post

---

Howard Simons is the managing editor of The Washington Post.

with common rules of practice about good writing and correct usage, abbreviations and capitalization, punctuation and spelling, headlines and datelines and deadlines and bylines.

This stylebook also is a time for renewal. Just as fashions change, so, too, does language usage. Descriptive words and phrases acceptable in an earlier time now are viewed as insensitive or, worse, pejorative. At the same time, once-precluded "four-letter words"—the euphemism for profane or obscene language—have raced into print. And there are new words and new phrases—Ms., chairperson—and the question of what to do about them.

Our stylebook concerns even more. For example, there is a chapter about fairness and conflicts of interest—aspects of journalism which have no Strunk or Fowler or Webster as guides. A body of ethics has evolved to govern the gathering and dissemination of the news—not necessarily objectively or subjectively, but fairly. Such a code, if that is the word, differs from newspaper to newspaper. This stylebook describes and prescribes ours.

There is a chapter on the media and the law and the continuing battle over the First Amendment.

There is, too, a chapter by our ombudsman, a piquant essay about the concept of an in-house critic and what that critic does for the newspaper and its readers.

Because Washington is both a city and a nation's capital, there are chapters about local government and federal government. The latter, particularly, is a political Baedeker.

Withal, the message of this book is essentially that there is no substitute for good writing. As Strunk put it:

"If those who have studied the art of writing are in accord on any one point, it is this: the surest way to arouse and hold the attention of the reader is by being specific, definite and concrete."

In sum, the rules in this book apply not just to Washington or The Washington Post. They are good rules for good usage in life and letters here and everywhere—just as a good newspaper is valuable beyond its immediate community.

Good taste, good grammar, good sense, good reporting, good writing—this is the stuff of style.

The Washington Post
DESKBOOK ON STYLE

BENJAMIN C. BRADLEE
STANDARDS AND ETHICS

The Washington Post is pledged to an aggressive, responsible and fair pursuit of the truth without fear of any special interest, and with favor to none.

Washington Post reporters and editors are pledged to approach every assignment with the fairness of open minds and without prior judgment. The search for opposing views must be routine. Comment from persons accused or chal-

---

Benjamin C. Bradlee is the executive editor of The Washington Post.

lenged in stories must be included. The motives of those who press their views upon us must routinely be examined, and it must be recognized that these motives can be noble and ignoble, obvious and ulterior.

We fully recognize that the power we have inherited as the monopoly morning newspaper in the capital of the free world carries with it special responsibilities:

- to listen to the voiceless
- to avoid any and all acts of arrogance
- to face the public with politeness and candor.

A. CONFLICT OF INTEREST

This newspaper is pledged to avoid conflict of interest or the appearance of conflict of interest, wherever or whenever possible. In particular:

- We pay our own way.
- We accept no gifts from news sources. Exceptions are minimal (tickets to cultural events to be reviewed) or obvious (invitations to meals). Occasionally, other exceptions might qualify. If in doubt, consult the executive editor or the managing editor or his deputy.
- We work for no one except The Washington Post without permission from supervisors, which will be granted in the rarest of circumstances.
- We free-lance for no one without permission from department heads. Permission will be granted only if The Post has no interest in the story, and only if it is to appear in a medium that does not compete with The Post.
- Many outside activities and jobs are incompatible with the proper performance of work on an independent newspaper. Connections with government are perhaps the most objectionable.

- We avoid any practice that interferes with our ability to report and present the news with independence.
- We make every reasonable effort to be free of obligation to news sources and to special interests.
- We avoid active involvement in causes of any kind— politics, community affairs, social action, demonstrations—that could compromise, or seem to compromise, our ability to report and edit with fairness. Relatives cannot fairly be subject to Post rules, but it should be recognized that their involvement in causes can at least appear to compromise our integrity.

B. THE REPORTER'S ROLE

Although it has become increasingly difficult for this newspaper and for the press generally to do so since Watergate, reporters should make every effort to remain in the audience, to stay off the stage, to report history, not to make history.

C. ERRORS

This newspaper is pledged to minimize errors, and to correct them when they occur. Accuracy is our goal; candor is our defense.

D. ATTRIBUTION OF SOURCES

This newspaper is pledged to disclose the source of all information unless disclosure would endanger the source's security. When we agree to protect a source's identity, that identity will not be made known to anyone outside The Post.

Before any information is accepted without full attribution, reporters must make every reasonable effort to get it on the record. If that is not possible, reporters should consider seeking the information elsewhere. If that in turn is not possible, reporters should request an on-the-record reason for restricting the source's identity, and should include the reason in the story.

In any case, some kind of identification is almost always possible—by department or by position, for example—and should be reported.

E. PLAGIARISM

Attribution of material from other newspapers and other media must be total. Plagiarism is one of journalism's unforgivable sins.

F. FAIRNESS

Reporters and editors of The Post are committed to fairness. While arguments about objectivity are endless, the concept of fairness is something that editors and reporters can easily understand and pursue. Fairness results from a few simple practices:

- No story is fair if it omits facts of major importance or significance. So fairness includes completeness.
- No story is fair if it includes essentially irrelevant information at the expense of significant facts. So fairness includes relevance.
- No story is fair if it consciously or unconsciously misleads or even deceives the reader. So fairness includes honesty—leveling with the reader.
- No story is fair if reporters hide their biases or emotions behind such subtly pejorative words as "refused," "despite," "admit," and "massive." So fairness requires straightforwardness ahead of flashiness.

Reporters and editors should routinely ask themselves at the end of every story: "Have I been as fair as I can be?"

G. OPINION

On this newspaper, the separation of news columns from the editorial and opposite-editorial pages is solemn and complete. This separation is intended to serve the reader, who is entitled to the facts in the news columns and to opinions on the editorial and "op-ed" pages. But nothing in this separation of function and powers is intended to eliminate from the news columns honest, in-depth reporting, or analysis, or commentary, when such departures from strictly factual reporting are plainly labeled.

H. THE NATIONAL AND COMMUNITY INTEREST

The Washington Post is vitally concerned with the national interest and with the community interest. We believe these interests are best served by the widest possible dissemination of information. The claim of national interest by a federal official does not automatically equate with the national interest. The claim of community interest by a local official does not automatically equate with the community interest.

I. TASTE

The Washington Post as a newspaper respects taste and decency, understanding that society's concepts of taste and decency are constantly changing. A word offensive to the last generation can be part of the next generation's common vocabulary. But we shall avoid prurience. We shall avoid profanities and obscenities unless their use is so essential to a story of significance that its meaning is lost without them. In no case shall obscenities be used without the approval of the executive editor or the managing editor or his deputy.

J. THE POST'S PRINCIPLES

After Eugene Meyer bought The Washington Post in

1933 and began the family ownership which continues today, he published "These Principles":

The first mission of a newspaper is to tell the truth as nearly as the truth may be ascertained.

The newspaper shall tell ALL the truth so far as it can learn it, concerning the important affairs of America and the world.

As a disseminator of the news, the paper shall observe the decencies that are obligatory upon a private gentleman.

What it prints shall be fit reading for the young as well as for the old.

The newspaper's duty is to its readers and to the public at large, and not to the private interests of its owner.

In the pursuit of truth, the newspaper shall be prepared to make sacrifice of its material fortunes, if such course be necessary for the public good.

The newspaper shall not be the ally of any special interest, but shall be fair and free and wholesome in its outlook on public affairs and public men.

"These Principles" are re-endorsed herewith.

CHRISTOPHER H. LITTLE

NEWSPAPER LAW AND FAIRNESS

A. *Libel*
B. *Invasion of privacy*
C. *Fair trial issues and crime reporting*
D. *Access to information*
E. *Legal terminology and usage*
F. *Subpoenas served on staff members*
G. *Court actions restricting publication or access*

In general: Laws and court rulings governing such matters as libel, invasion of privacy and freedom of information have changed significantly in recent years and almost certainly will continue to change. When there is any doubt whatsoever about the law and its application to their stories and professional activities, reporters and editors must consult immediately with the departmental editor and, if necessary, with Post counsel.

Christopher H. Little is counsel for The Washington Post.

A. LIBEL

1. What is libelous?

Basically, a libelous statement is a published statement that injures a person (or organization or corporation) in his trade, profession or community standing. For example, it is normally "libelous" to publish a statement that a person is incompetent in his profession, that a person is a bigamist or that a person or organization sells products or raises funds under false pretenses. If the published statement is not true, and none of the other legal justifications for publishing a libelous statement are applicable, the person or organization may successfully bring a libel suit to recover for damages resulting from the publication.

2. Truth.

The truth may injure a person's reputation and therefore technically be "libelous," but a person cannot successfully bring a libel suit for damages resulting from publication of the truth. For example, it is libelous to state that a person has been convicted of shoplifting; but if it is true that the person has been convicted of shoplifting, he or she cannot successfully sue the paper for libel for publishing that fact.

3. Reasonable care.

There will inevitably be instances in which a newspaper has a reasonable basis for believing that a statement is true, but discovers after publication that the statement was not in fact true. Supreme Court opinions indicate that a newspaper will still be able to defend itself successfully against a libel suit if it can prove that it took reasonable care in the preparation of the article involved, and was not negligent in making the false statement. In other words, the same care that is required by responsible journalism will stand a reporter in good stead on questions of libel.

4. Public officials and public figures—the New York Times rule.

The Supreme Court's New York Times rule was first established in the case of *Times v. Sullivan* in 1964. In that case, the court held that when a newspaper publishes a false libelous statement about a public official (in that case, an Alabama city aide), the First and 14th amendments to the United States Constitution bar a libel judgment in favor of the public official—unless the official can prove that the newspaper knew that the statement was false or printed it in reckless disregard of its truth or falsity. The New York Times rule has since been extended to statements concerning "public figures" who are not public officials.

One difficulty in applying this rule comes in determining whether a person is a "public official." It seems clear that elected officials such as legislators and council members are "public officials" within the New York Times rule. Appointed officials such as Cabinet officers and heads of government agencies or departments also normally come within the rule. Court opinions have in some cases extended the reach of the rule to relatively low-level civil servants. But the lower the level of the official and the more ministerial the job, the less likely the possibility that a court will apply the "public official" label to the person.

It is even more difficult to determine whether a person is a "public figure," and while some people are public figures for all libel law purposes, some may be public figures only for limited purposes. In

1974, in the case of *Gertz v. Welch*, the Supreme Court decided that a Chicago lawyer who was acting as counsel in a well-publicized case and who had been involved in a number of civic activities was not a public figure. More recently, in *Time v. Firestone*, 1976, the court held that a prominent socialite who was involved in a notorious divorce suit was not a public figure. The court in *Firestone* indicated that factors which might be considered in deciding whether a person is a public figure include whether an issue of "public affairs" is involved and whether the person has voluntarily injected himself or herself into the issue involved.

Even if it is clear that a person against whom allegations are made is a public official or public figure, this does not mean that a reporter can abandon ordinary care in checking the story. The New York Times rule is a constitutional means of protecting a free and independent press. It is not an excuse for sloppy journalism.

5. Consent.

Another defense to a libel action is the consent of the person libeled to publication of the libelous material. However, keep in mind that the person might later deny having given consent. If you are relying on consent as your defense, don't accept oral consent without witnesses—as in a two-party telephone conversation. Get the consent in writing or at least before witnesses you can rely on.

6. Other defenses.

There are other legal defenses to libel actions, but they vary from state to state and cannot be generalized here. What must be understood is that each story presents a unique situation in terms of all the circumstances involved. There is no magic formula by which a statement can be judged to determine whether a suit will result from its publication or whether a suit would be successful.

Again, the best way of avoiding libel problems is through the use of solid journalistic techniques and a sense of fairness. The same careful evaluation and checking of sources and the same concern for precise use of language which make for responsible journalism will also take care of most potential libel problems.

It is particularly important to obtain, whenever possible, the response of a person against whom allegations are made. Sometimes this will lead to new information that changes the thrust of the story. If allegations are made, responses should run in the same story if possible.

This does not mean that a story cannot be run until a response is obtained. If the person involved refuses to respond to repeated telephone calls or refuses to make a statement, this fact can be noted in the story.

7. Republication of libel.

Care and sense of fairness cannot be abandoned when the libelous statement is quoted from a person or from another publication. As a general rule, the republication of a libelous statement is no different for purposes of libel law than the initiation of a libelous statement. What is necessary is an independent evaluation of the accuracy of the libelous statement.

8. Court proceedings.

An area which often raises libel questions is the reporting of court proceedings. Because reporting of these proceedings often involves statements which are potentially very damaging to the persons involved, they should be treated with particular care. Be sure you have all the names right. Papers filed with a court and opinions of a court should be precisely described. Often, it is desirable to use direct quotations from court filings or opinions so that the question of an erroneous interpretation does not come up. When charges contained in a court paper are reported, the response of the person libeled to each charge should be included if at all possible.

Other special considerations in the reporting of court cases are discussed in Sections B and C, Invasion of Privacy and Fair Trial Issues and Crime Reporting.

9. Captions and headlines.

The same preciseness and care that go into stories should go into captions and headlines. In particular, if the subject matter of a story poses a possible libel problem, the supervising editor should see that care is taken in reviewing any captions and headlines associated with the story—even if the story as written avoids potential libel problems.

10. Review of potential libel problems.

When a reporter is working with material that may pose a libel problem, the story and all the issues should be taken to a supervising editor. The supervising editor will decide whether to ask counsel to review the story.

11. General policy.

Finally, we should make every reasonable effort not only to assure accuracy and meet the minimum requirements of libel law, but also to produce stories which are balanced, fair and in good taste, and in keeping with our own high professional standards.

B. INVASION OF PRIVACY

Courts or legislatures in a number of states have recognized the right of individuals to recover damages for some form of "invasion of privacy." Invasion of privacy is not a single, clearly defined right of action, but rather a collection of legal theories which vary widely in their application from state to state. Cases recognizing the concept of invasion of privacy generally fall into four categories—"appropriation," "intrusion," "public disclosure of private facts" and "false light in the public eye."

1. Appropriation.

   A number of courts have awarded damages for the appropriation of a person's name or likeness. This can cover appropriation for commercial purposes (such as using a person's face in an advertisement without permission) or for noncommercial purposes (such as impersonation of a person to obtain secret information or use of a person's name in a political endorsement without permission). Liability under this theory does not extend to situations where a person's name or photograph is used in a news story.

2. Intrusion.

   A number of cases have recognized as an invasion of privacy various types of intrusion into a person's seclusion or private affairs, without regard to publication. The cases have included physical intrusion into a home or hotel room, electronic eavesdropping, unauthorized search of private papers, use of high-powered binoculars to see into someone's home and the unauthorized taking of photographs in private places. Normally, no problem is presented with the taking and publication of photographs in public places, although there may be an exception when a photograph places a person in an extremely embarrassing light and no newsworthy event is involved. If a photograph may be such an exception, or a photograph is taken in a private place, the persons photographed should be asked to sign a publication release form like the one (Figure 1) on Page 15 before the photograph is published.

Criminal statutes prohibit certain types of "intrusion" involving the use of tape recorders or other electronic means of picking up conversations. If a reporter wishes to tape-record a conversation without the permission of all persons involved in the conversation, the reporter should first consult the departmental editor, who will discuss it with counsel for the paper before proceeding. Of course, a reporter has the right without consultation with an editor to use a tape recorder at a public press conference.

3. Public disclosure of private facts.
On occasion, a court has allowed recovery of damages on the ground of invasion of privacy when embarrassing or confidential information has been made public. This theory normally does not apply to matters of public record, although in one California case the court allowed recovery against a newspaper which published an article discussing an 11-year-old conviction of a hijacker who had since been rehabilitated. When embarrassing or very private information is published as something other than "hard" news, consideration should be given to potential legal problems.

The most frequent problem in this area for a newspaper is the reporting of sex crimes. It is the policy of The Post not to publish the names of surviving victims of sex crimes. If in a particular case there is some extraordinary reason for an exception to this policy, it should be discussed with the managing editor, who will discuss it with counsel.

FIGURE 1—Photo Release Form

The Washington Post

1150 15TH STREET, N. W.
WASHINGTON, D. C. 20071
(202) 223-6000

Date _____

I (We) hereby consent to the reproduction in The Washington Post of a
photograph of

(Describe) _____

_____

_____

Parent, Guardian or Agency Head

Witness or other signatory

Special care should be taken in reporting the name of a juvenile (under age 18) charged with a crime. As a general rule, the name should not be reported. A reporter's supervising editor should be consulted before the name is used.

4. False light in the public eye.
The "false light" cases have upheld a claim of invasion of privacy when the plaintiff has been wrongly associated with an objectionable matter.

Usually, this question arises in connection with photographs used to illustrate feature stories. For example, a photograph of a couple used to illustrate a story on "the wrong kind of love," a photograph of an honest taxi driver accompanying an article on dishonest taxi drivers and a photograph of an innocent traffic accident victim used to illustrate an article on careless pedestrians have all been held to place the plaintiff in a false light in the public eye and therefore to constitute an invasion of privacy. The false light problem can also arise when fictionalized references to actual persons are published.

As in the case of libel law, a reporter's best protection against invasion-of-privacy charges is the use of responsible journalistic techniques. Care in the use of photographs, responsible news-gathering methods and the use of taste and judgment will help to keep a newspaper out of the vague and troublesome area of invasion of privacy.

C. FAIR TRIAL ISSUES AND CRIME REPORTING

We should take care to report crime news with caution and accuracy, to bear in mind the rights of the accused and to leave the deciding of guilt or innocence to the courts. Be especially careful about these points:

1. Guilt of accused or arrested persons must not be conveyed or implied in the stories or headlines. Words that connote guilt or imply conviction should not be used.

2. Statements to police officers, reporters or prosecutors are not confessions. The term *confession* should not

be used either in headlines or text unless we are dealing with an acknowledgment of guilt given by a defendant in a courtroom. Accused persons *state, relate, report, explain* or otherwise elaborate upon a criminal situation in remarks to police. We prefer to avoid the use of even such words as *admit* or *acknowledge.*

3. Reports of trials should accurately reflect the proceedings. Reporters and editors should give the prosecution and the defense fair coverage.

4. Identification in crime stories must be strictly accurate when reporting initials, address and place of employment. If names are not used in a crime story and a general address is given, care should be taken that a cloud of suspicion and guilt is not thrown over all the residents of a building or a neighborhood, employees of a firm or inmates of an institution.

5. Crime stories should not give such detailed descriptions of how a crime was committed as to constitute a handbook for criminal enterprise.

6. Persons charged with a violation of the law should be given the opportunity to reply to such charges, if possible.

7. Do not routinely report arrest records of suspects in crime stories. In some circumstances, however, a record is relevant and adds materially to the interest of the story. A record (and it should include disposition) may be used only after clearance with a departmental editor. Particular effort should be made to avoid prejudicing a trial by publishing the record of a suspect immediately before trial.

8. We avoid publishing pictures that might prejudice

the trial of defendants. Photographs that show a subject manacled, disheveled, beaten, or pinioned by attendants should be avoided, although we do publish such pictures where the arrest process is newsworthy, as when there is police or citizen action at the moment of capture. Police identification should be removed from "mug" shots.

9. Sex discrimination has no more place in crime stories than anywhere else in a paper. In particular, stories dealing with prostitution raids must refer to all charged—the prostitutes, their procurers and their customers.

10. As a general rule, we name persons charged with crimes. However, in "trend" or "survey" stories, where one or a few cases are selected as examples, the departmental editor should carefully weigh whether to use those names—particularly if they would not have otherwise seen print.

11. Do not call a person an alleged murderer or the crime murder unless so charged; a person may be an alleged killer, an alleged slayer, an alleged strangler, and the deed may be manslaughter or even self-defense.

12. The expression *convicted murderer* (or *convicted rapist* and the like) is acceptable after conviction and exhaustion of appeals; but after conviction and before appeals have been exhausted, say the prisoner has been *convicted of murder* and if an appeal has been filed, say so. Do not use *accused murderer* or the like; rephrase and say *charged with murder.*

13. Do not use *not guilty,* since the word *not* might be accidentally dropped in typesetting; use *innocent* instead. This applies, for example, to a plea of *not guilty* as well as to a jury verdict.

D. ACCESS TO INFORMATION

All reporters and editors should be familiar with directives and laws governing freedom of information. At The Post they are on file in the library.

1. Freedom of Information Act, 1967 federal law.
   a. The Freedom of Information Act requires that all records of a federal agency be made available to the public unless the records fall within certain specific exceptions. The exceptions include classified documents, trade secrets and certain internal decision-making documents. Counsel for The Post, or your paper, can be consulted when a question arises as to the requirements of the act in a particular case.
   b. All federal agencies must make available for inspection and copying: all final opinions, both concurring and dissenting; statements of policy and interpretation not published in the *Federal Register*, and staff manuals and instructions affecting the public unless promptly offered for sale.
   c. Agencies may delete "identifying details" to prevent unwarranted invasion of privacy but must justify it in writing.
   d. Agencies must maintain an index of "any matter" issued, adopted or promulgated after June 4, 1967.
   e. Agencies must make records promptly available to everyone in accordance with published rules for time, fees, place and procedure. Form letters for requesting information under the act are available.
   f. Agencies must keep records of final votes by all members in all proceedings and make them available for inspection.

g. A sample form for requesting information under the Freedom of Information Act (Figure 2) is on Page 21.

2. Freedom of information laws in the District of Columbia, Maryland and Virginia.

   a. The District of Columbia has a Freedom of Information Act modeled on the federal act. It provides generally that records maintained by the District of Columbia government are available for inspection or copying. The exceptions to this general rule are similar to the exceptions of the federal statute. Requests for access should be made to the department which keeps the records. Different departments may have their own regulations on procedures to be followed when making a request. The District government is supposed to take action on a request within 10 working days. If a request is denied, the denial can be appealed to the mayor. If the mayor upholds the denial, his decision can be challenged in Superior Court.

   b. The Virginia Freedom of Information Act is much less complex. It provides generally that official records of state or local government bodies shall be open, with a few specific exceptions such as materials prepared for use in litigation and materials furnished in confidence to a government body.

   c. Maryland's statute is also fairly brief and also generally requires that public records be open. However, it contains a longer list of specific exceptions to the general rule. Requests for inspection or copying are to be directed to the custodian of the records.

FIGURE 2—Request for Information Under Freedom of Information Act

FREEDOM OF INFORMATION ACT
Initial Request Letter

Dear (person designated in agency regulations):

Pursuant to the Freedom of Information Act, 5 U.S.C. § 552, as amended, I hereby request disclosure of the following records for inspection and possible copying:

(List documents with identifying descriptions as full and specific as possible.)

If you regard any records in the foregoing list as exempt from required disclosure under the Act, I hereby request that you exercise your discretion to disclose them nevertheless.

I further request that you disclose the listed documents as they become available to you, without waiting until all the documents have been assembled.

I am making this request on behalf of The Washington Post, a newspaper of general circulation in the Washington, D.C. metropolitan area and throughout the United States. The records disclosed pursuant to this request will be used in the preparation of news articles for dissemination to the public. Accordingly, I request that, pursuant to 5 U.S.C. § 552(a)(4)(A), you waive all fees in the public interest because the furnishing of the information sought by this request will primarily benefit the public. If, however, you decline to waive all fees, I am prepared to pay your normal search fees (and copying fees if I decide to copy any records), but I request that you notify me if you expect your search fees to exceed $_____.

I look forward to hearing from you promptly.

Sincerely,

Appeal Letter

Dear (person designated in agency regulations to hear appeals):

On ___(date)_____ I requested disclosure of certain records of your agency under the Freedom of Information Act, 5 U.S.C. § 552. The records sought are listed in the letter of request, which is attached. On _____(date)_____ the request was denied. A copy of the denial is attached. I hereby appeal from the denial of the request. I also request that you exercise your discretion to disclose any records which you may regard as exempt from required disclosure under the Act.

I look forward to hearing from you promptly.

Sincerely,

3. Washington Metropolitan Police Department, 1968 directive.
   a. The following information must be released at the scene of an incident or by officials handling the report:
      • Names of individuals involved (although the press usually does not use names of female sex-crime victims, juveniles or witnesses and usually withholds names of the dead until relatives have been notified).
      • Description, age, address and other pertinent information about those involved.
      • Such information about the incident as time, place, weapons used and items seized.
   b. Information and access to the scene may be restricted if necessary for the success of the investigation.
   c. The following information may not be released except as part of a record open to the public:
      • Arrest records.
      • Personal opinions about a person's character or record.
      • Admissions or confessions.
   d. The following police records are open to inspection:
      • General complaint files.
      • Arrest books containing: case number and date and time of arrest . . . name, address, birthdate, color, birthplace, occupation and marital status of persons arrested . . . offense charged and place arrested . . . name and address of complainant . . . name of arresting officer . . . case disposition.
      • Records of lost, missing and stolen property.

- Personnel record of each member of the department.
4. Department of Defense, 1963 directive.
   a. When accidents occur on military bases, identities of dead and injured will be withheld until relatives are notified, but officials will try to release such information as soon as possible.
   b. When accidents occur outside military bases, identities of dead and injured will be released immediately except in remote air crashes not involving civilian casualties.
   c. When accidents involve classified material, the press will be advised that reporting on or photographing such material is illegal. Civilian authorities will be asked to prevent the compromising of such material and to recover any material taken.

E. LEGAL TERMINOLOGY AND USAGE
1. Be careful about the phrase *the court held*. A holding is the law laid down, not the language of the judge.
2. Be accurate in describing the law laid down. Don't use *unconstitutional* when you mean *illegal*.
3. Be careful about the terms *confess, convicted* and *accused*, as noted in C2 and C12 of this chapter.
4. The correct term is either *Chief Justice of the United States* or *Chief Justice* but never *Chief Justice of the Supreme Court* or *Justice*.
5. In reporting a prison sentence (such as *five to 15 years*), also say when the person will be eligible for parole (such as *after three years*).
6. Avoid legal jargon where possible; when it is essential to use a term such as *in camera, ex parte* or *nol pros*, follow it with a synonym in parentheses.

7. There often is confusion among three important Supreme Court rulings on the rights of defendants. Clear explanation in news stories can help prevent this. The three:

   a. *Gideon v. Wainwright*, 1963. The Supreme Court required states to provide indigent defendants with lawyers in all felony cases.

   b. *Escobedo v. Illinois*, 1964. The Supreme Court said police must permit a defendant to consult a lawyer promptly after arrest.

   c. *Miranda v. Arizona*, 1966. The Supreme Court required police to immediately notify a suspect of the right to consult an attorney and to remain silent during interrogation.

F. SUBPOENAS SERVED ON STAFF MEMBERS

Any effort to subpoena a reporter, or to discuss a case with a reporter as part of preparing the case, presents very serious First Amendment problems. The First Amendment right to publish newspapers means little if the government, through the instrument of the courts, can interfere with the ability of the press to gather the news.

Testimony by reporters in court cases concerning their news-gathering activities will discourage many persons from talking freely to reporters, because they will be afraid that what they say may end up in litigation. This is particularly true in a case where a reporter is asked to reveal a confidential source or information provided in confidence. But it is also true when a reporter is asked to provide nonconfidential information. The mere fact that a reporter appears on the witness stand to testify concerning his or her news gathering has a chilling effect on many potential sources of information.

The First Amendment protection of news gathering

has been recognized in a number of recent cases in which subpoenas seeking to compel reporters to testify have been struck down. In particular, there has been a tendency by the courts to recognize the First Amendment right of the reporter not to testify in cases where the information sought by the subpoena can be obtained by an alternative means.

Subpoenas on reporters or editors may also raise the problem of intrusion into the editorial process. Inquiries into information gathered by a reporter which has not been included in a story and questions about a reporter's notes or the editing of a story intrude into the right of a free press to make its own editorial and reporting judgments without being second-guessed in a court proceeding.

Despite these serious First Amendment concerns, in some cases reporters have been ordered by a judge to testify. Reporters in a number of these cases have elected to go to jail for contempt rather than testify.

The Post, as will most responsible newspapers, backs any reporter who is subpoenaed. This newspaper has a long-standing practice of resisting subpoenas directed to reporters where possible. If a lawyer for either side asks a staff member to testify or wants to talk to the staff member, the staff member should say nothing in reply other than, "I will have our counsel call you." Then the staff member should immediately notify the departmental editor, who, in turn, will promptly call counsel and discuss the situation. This will avoid making it more difficult for The Post to resist such attempts. Any information given out will make it more difficult to resist the subpoena. Therefore, staff members should not talk to the lawyer at all. In particular, they should not say whom they talked to, whether they have any notes or even that they remember the story or stand by it.

They should SAY NOTHING except, "I have to talk to my editors and lawyers."

G. COURT ACTIONS RESTRICTING PUBLICATION OR ACCESS

1. Prior restraint on publication.

The Supreme Court's 1976 decision in *Nebraska Press Association v. Stuart* held that a court order seeking to prevent the media from publishing certain types of information from a murder trial violated the First Amendment. The case was a landmark decision, because it made clear that a judge concerned about assuring a fair trial should use methods such as jury sequestration rather than prior restraints on the press. Indeed, it appears that a majority of the court will hold that the First Amendment prohibits any prior restraints on publication except when an immediate national security danger is involved, such as publication of sailing times of ships during time of war.

2. "Gag" orders directed against persons other than the press.

The Nebraska case decision does not necessarily prevent a court from ordering persons under its jurisdiction, such as prosecution and defense attorneys, not to discuss a pending case with the press. Thus, even though a court cannot prevent the press from printing what appears on the public record in a trial, or indeed anything it discovers about the trial from public or confidential sources, a court may attempt to limit publicity about a case by restricting sources of information. Normally, these gag orders are directed against counsel and parties to the case. However, they are sometimes also directed against witnesses. If a reporter or editor learns of a gag

order which seems to be unnecessarily broad or restrictive, counsel should be consulted to determine whether a challenge to the gag order is appropriate.
3. Access to court proceedings and court records
From time to time, a court may seek to reduce publicity about a case by closing a court proceeding or by sealing certain court records. Any such effort raises serious First Amendment problems. The Post has been successful in a number of cases in defeating efforts to close all or part of a court proceeding or record. If a reporter or an editor encounters a situation in which court records or proceedings are being closed, counsel should be consulted to determine whether a challenge to the action is appropriate.

CHARLES SEIB

THE OMBUDSMAN: SAUCE FOR THE GANDER

The news business is becoming increasingly uneasy about a paradox in its relationship with the other institutions of society.

The news media are, we say, essential to the system as relayers of information and as watchdogs. Only if we effectively fill those roles will citizens be informed and will the system work. We do this under the protection of the First Amendment, interpreted as a broad guarantee that the press can operate without interference. Which brings us to the paradox:

The press, clearly one of society's most powerful institutions, is alone among those institutions in being exempt from the kind of scrutiny and whistle-blowing it imposes on the others.

This paradox is no new thing. More than 50 years ago, Walter Lippmann, journalism's philosopher, was troubled by it. "There is everywhere an increasingly angry disillusionment about the press, a growing sense of being baffled

---

Charles Seib became the Washington Post ombudsman in 1974. Before that he was the managing editor of The Washington Star.

and misled," he wrote then. " . . . If publishers and authors themselves do not face the facts and attempt to deal with them, some day Congress, in a fit of temper, egged on by an outraged public opinion, will operate on the press with an ax."

He declared that "what is sauce for the goose—that is to say for public men, business men, bankers, labor leaders, artists—must be sauce for the gander, for reporters, editors, commentators, book reviewers, dramatic critics." The lack of open criticism of the press, he said, "deprives the press itself of the benefits of the very principle of which the press is, in relation to everything else, the chief exponent."

So that is the problem—long-standing but increasingly embarrassing. What is the solution? Several approaches have been tried. There is the National News Council, which is still groping for a viable role as a monitor of the media. There are regional news councils. And then there is the ombudsman, the internal monitor of the individual newspaper. That's the approach we are using at The Post.

The first Post ombudsman was appointed in 1970. He and his two immediate successors were members of the news staff. The present ombudsman was hired from outside The Post and was given a five-year contract with the understanding that it would not be renewed. In addition to guaranteeing his independence, the contract has two other advantages: It provides financial protection for the ombudsman should The Post decide to fire him, and it establishes that he is an outsider with neither a past nor a future at The Post.

The ombudsman operates this way:

His job, as he sees it, is to represent The Post's readers and to react to the paper himself as a reader. He handles complaints from readers on matters of fairness, accuracy, balance and professional standards. In addition, he criticizes the paper on the basis of his own observations.

The product is a stream of memos—an average of three or four a week, most of them dealing with several subjects—to the executive editor and the managing editor. The memos relay reader complaints (and often the ombudsman's comments on their validity and on what might be done about them) as well as his own criticisms.

All aspects of the news and editorial content of the paper are fair game: a headline that is obscure or ungrammatical or that overstates a story, a lead that stretches the facts beyond reason, an overplay or underplay, inaccuracies of every kind—in other words, all the sins to which journalism is heir.

The memos are not secret. Copies are distributed to all the assistant managing editors, for use as they see fit, and they are available to anyone on the editorial staff who wants to read them.

The ombudsman has an important additional function. He sometimes goes public. That is, when he feels it is appropriate he writes a column for the Op Ed page in which he deals with The Post's handling—or mishandling—of the news.

These columns, which are in addition to a weekly news business column on the same page, are prompted by one of two reasons: The ombudsman feels that a published column is the only way to redress a wrong done by The Post, or he feels that the column will be of interest to a public that has been poorly informed about how the press operates. Sometimes the column is a result of a disagreement between the ombudsman and The Post's editors. It is, in effect, his ultimate weapon as the representative and protector of the paper's readers and the public.

Always the ombudsman tries to maintain his status as an outsider. He does not attend the daily conferences of editors, nor does he take part in policy discussions. He picks up the paper each morning as a reader, with no commitments to the decisions made the night before.

Does the ombudsman system work? Yes, but I'm not sure how well. The presence of someone to whom readers can bring their complaints for a sympathetic hearing has obvious advantages for both the readers and the paper. I think also that the presence of an ombudsman has heightened the staff's sensitivity toward fairness and accuracy and clarity and of the dangers of overkill.* On the other hand, there is no evidence that he is, or can be, a journalistic cure-all.

Does the presence of an ombudsman have any harmful effects? Does it upset the staff to have a second-guesser, hired from outside The Post, on the premises? News people are traditionally sensitive to criticism, particularly in print. They dish it out with flair, but they don't take it very well. This is partly because until recently they haven't had to; systematic criticism of the press in the press is relatively new.

Nevertheless, I have no reason to believe that my presence is disruptive or that the possible harmful effects—damaged staff morale or the resentment accorded a second-guesser, for example—outweigh the benefits.

*A collection of columns and internal memoranda written by ombudsmen of The Washington Post has been published under the title *Of the Press, By the Press, For the Press (& Others, Too)*, second edition, edited by Laura Longley Babb; illustrated. (Boston: Houghton Mifflin, 1976.)

IV TASTE AND SENSIBILITIES

In general: Each of us has been offended at times by slurs against our age, race, religion or sex. When lapses in taste and fairness and sensitivity occur in public and in print, they do more than offend; they create prejudice and reinforce stereotypes.

A. AGE

1. Mention a person's age in stories when it is relevant, particularly if it helps to identify or describe a person. But do not mention a person's age simply because you know it or to pad out a short headline.

2. Generally let age speak for itself. Such terms as *youngster, teen-ager, middle-aged, retiree* and *senior citizen* are imprecise and, to some, derogatory. So they should be used with care. The legal age for adulthood, for example, is 18.

B. COURTESY TERMS AND PROFESSIONAL TITLES

1. Use *Mr., Mrs.* and *Miss* only in obituaries, in reference to couples, in direct quotations and where essential for effect, as in editorials and critiques. In particular, do not use the terms with surnames after first reference.

   > *Mr. White died . . . ; Mr. and Mrs. Black filed the suit . . . ; the senator insisted he is "still a friend of Mrs. White"; The Post believes Mr. Black owes an explanation. (But: White told the committee she will . . . ; Black and the first lady stood . . . ; in his sermon, White urged . . .)*

2. Refer to married women by their first names and surnames and without the term *Mrs.* unless only the husband's first name is known. Refer to single women by their first names and surnames without the term *Miss.* Do not use the term *Ms.* except in direct quotations or in discussing the term itself.

   > *Helen Black* (Married), not *Mrs. John Black* (unless her first name is not known); *Mary White* (unmarried), not *Miss Mary White*

3. Use civic, military and professional titles as infrequently as possible after first reference.

Black (not *Gen. Black*) *testified that . . .*

4. Do not use titles standing alone unless necessary for clarity, emphasis or effect.

White (not *the secretary*) *told the committee. . . .* (But: *It was sent to the secretary rather than the under secretary; The secretary and the senators debated for two hours.*)

5. Use the title *Dr.* for practitioners of the healing arts (including chiropractors and osteopaths) but not for holders of PhDs or honorary degrees.

6. When relevant, and if possible, specify the kind of doctor the person is.

Dr. John Black, an internist (an orthodontist, a chiropractor), . . .

C. DIALECT

1. Use dialect in quotations only when relevant. The mere fact that a person speaks with a twang, drawl or ethnic accent or uses bad grammar or inappropriate language has no bearing on most stories.

2. Although direct quotations must not be altered, such pronunciations as *Ah* and *runnin'* in most cases can and should be written as *I* and *running*.

D. IDENTIFICATION OF JUVENILES

1. Generally do not use the names of juveniles (those younger than age 18) at the time of arrest or in connection with judicial proceedings unless otherwise directed by a departmental editor.

2. Names may be used when juveniles are remanded for trial as adults.

3. When names are withheld, be careful to avoid inadvertent identification by description.

4. Unless it is essential to the understanding of a story, do not mention the adoptive status of a child.

E. IDENTIFICATION OF RACE

1. Avoid identifying race or ethnic background unless the information is relevant. It may be so:

a. In stories involving politics, social action, social conditions, achievement and other matters where race can be a distinguishing factor.

b. Where usage has sanctioned the description: *black leader, Irish tenor, Polish wedding.*

c. In reporting an incident that cannot be satisfactorily explained without reference to race. However, the mere fact than an incident involves persons of different races does not, of itself, mean that racial tags should be used. And when racial identification is used, the races of all involved should be mentioned.

2. Do not mention a person's race in describing criminal suspects or fugitives unless the rest of the description is detailed enough to be meaningful. Sketchy descriptions are often meaningless and may apply to large numbers of innocent persons.

3. When referring to people of Spanish or Portuguese blood, the terms *Hispano, Hispanic* and *Hispano-American* are preferable to *Latin, Latino, Chicano* and *Spanish American.* (Technically, persons of Portuguese blood are *Luso-Americans,* but the term is not familiar enough for newspaper use.) The terms *Latin American, Central American* and *South American* may be used in a geographic sense. The terms *Mexican American, Portuguese American,* etc. are always valid when referring to dual heritage. The term *Spanish American* is acceptable when referring to culture, food and the like. Puerto Ricans should be called *Puerto Ricans* rather than *Hispano-Americans* (which suggests a southwestern U.S. heritage); how-ever, Puerto Rican culture may be described as *Span-ish* or *Hispanic*.

F. NAMES AND INITIALS

1. Few errors can cause more damage or embarrassment (to the subject and to the paper) than a wrong or misspelled name. Be certain that identification and spelling are correct.
2. If confusion with another person is possible, clarify with identifying information.

    Jones is no relation to the prizefighter of the same name.
3. Use a first or middle initial, or a middle name, if it is the person's known preference or if doing so helps to identify the person. (However, the person's age or address is probably more widely known than his initial.)
4. Foreign names present special problems.
    a. Chinese usage generally puts the family name first *(Mao Tse-tung, Mao)*. But some Chinese have westernized their names *(Dr. Tsing-fu Tsiang, Tsiang)*.
    b. Many Indonesians have just one name—such as *President Suharto*.
    c. Some Koreans put family names first *(Kim Il Sung, Kim)* and some put them last *(Tongsun Park, Park)*; but in either case, the name is not hyphenated.
    d. Spanish and other Hispanic usage is more com-plex.
        • Most Hispanic men use the father's last name and then the mother's, sometimes with *y* (and)

between the names. In second reference, only the father's name is used.

> *Raul Jimenez Lopez (Jiminez); Joaquin Ortega*
> *y Castro (Ortega)*

- But some use both family names (because the father's is very common) or hyphenate the names.

> *Marco Perez Jiminez (Perez Jiminez), Hector*
> *Garcia-Godoy (Garcia-Godoy)*

- When a Hispanic woman marries, she retains her family name. *Maria Perez*, upon marrying *Luis Gonzalez*, becomes *Maria Perez de Gonzalez*. In Hispanic countries she would generally be known as *Sra. de Gonzalez*, but in this country she may choose to style herself as *Maria Gonzalez* and *Mrs. Gonzalez*. The Hispanic forms of the surname should be used if no special preference is known.

G. OBITUARIES

1. The Post's policy is to publish, whenever possible, all volunteered obituaries and photographs.
2. Deaths must be verified by the appropriate funeral home.
3. Obituaries should use the name the person used or was known by and should include the age, cause of death, names of immediate survivors and, if possible, some interesting facts regarding the person's life. Unsavory details need not be suppressed but should be placed in perspective.
4. Use *Mr., Mrs.* or *Miss* in all obituary references to the deceased.
5. Do not include specific addresses of the deceased. Use

the form *the 900 block of Florida avenue* if an address is necessary.

H. PROFANITY AND OBSCENITIES

1. Although profanity and obscenity have become much more widely used in recent years than heretofore, both publicly and in mixed company, their use in a family newspaper can seldom be justified.

2. Profanities and obscenities should not be used in a story unless something significant would otherwise be lost. The test should be "why use it?" rather than "why not use it?"

3. The simple fact that a person used a profanity or obscenity is not in itself justification for printing it. However, it may be used if:

   a. It reflects a mood or frame of mind that can be conveyed in no other way (as with John F. Kennedy's reference to steel executives as "sons of bitches" and John Dean's reference to "screwing" the Nixon administration's enemies).

   b. If the words themselves play a role in the story (as in reports about Supreme Court obscenity rulings).

4. When such use is deemed essential, simple profanities should be spelled out but "hard-core" obscenities referring to the body and sexual and excretory functions should use the *s---* form, which serves the purpose of communicating without jarring sensibilities any more than necessary.

5. The same rules apply to descriptive passages and photos. Detailed descriptions of a pornographic film or use of nude pictures can be justified only if they provide significant information or understanding that would otherwise be lacking in the story.

6. Questions regarding individual cases should be referred to the department editor.

I. RELIGION

1. Writers sometimes needlessly offend members of religious groups by failing to use correct terminology. It is a good rule of thumb to identify religious figures and organizations as they identify themselves. Consult the *Yearbook of American and Canadian Churches* and the *Official Catholic Directory*.

2. Christian usage

   a. Generally use clerical titles only in first reference. However, titles may be used in subsequent reference in quotations and stylized writing. Preferred subsequent-reference forms are listed below; avoid the forms *Mr. Black, Rev. Black* and *the Rev. Black* except in direct quotations.

   b. *The Rev.* is used in first reference for leaders of most Christian congregations. In subsequent references, Catholics use the form *Father Black* and Lutherans use the form *Pastor Black*.

   c. *The Most Rev.* is used in first reference for Roman Catholic bishops and archbishops and for Episcopal archbishops.

   d. *The Right Rev.* is used for Roman Catholic abbots and Episcopal bishops.

   e. *The Very Rev.* is used for deans of Anglican cathedrals and seminaries, priests who head most Roman Catholic seminaries and many priests of the Dominican order.

   f. *The Rev. Msgr.* (and then *Msgr.*) is used for Roman Catholic monsignors.

   g. *Cardinal* precedes the surname.
      William Cardinal Baum, Cardinal Baum

   h. United Methodist bishops are always just *Bishop*.

   i. Do not use *the Rev.* when referring to the spiritual leaders of the Church of Christ, Scientist (Christian Scientists), the Church of Jesus Christ of Latter-day Saints (Mormons), the Reorganized Church of Jesus Christ of Latter Day Saints (not Mormons, and note the difference in punctuation), the Churches of Christ and Jehovah's Witnesses.

j. The spiritual leader of Roman Catholic congregations (except cathedrals, which are led by *rectors*) and of most Protestant congregations is a *pastor*; Episcopal congregations are led by *rectors*, *vicars* or *priests-in-charge*; congregations of the United Church of Christ and of the Unitarian Universalist Association are led by *ministers*.

k. Priests, brothers and nuns often append initials to their names indicating their religious community. The Post does not use initials, but indicates the community membership in the body of the story.
Brother Joseph Davis of the National Office for Black Catholics, who is a Marist brother, . . .

3. Jewish usage

a. Judaism is divided into three main movements—Orthodox, Conservative and Reform (not Reformed)—and it is sometimes relevant to specify to which tradition a Jewish newsmaker belongs.

b. Only Reform Jews refer to their synagogues as temples; most Conservative and Orthodox Jews find that usage offensive.

c. A rabbi is the spiritual leader, not the pastor, of a Jewish congregation. A rabbi, incidentally, is a teacher, not a clergyman.

d. The Post conforms to the practice of the Jewish Community Council of Greater Washington in spelling the names of the principal Jewish holidays:
Hanukah, Passover, Purim, Rosh Hashanah, Shavuot, Sukkot and *Yom Kippur*

4. Miscellany.
  a. Spell it *Moslem,* not *Muslim.* The religion itself is called *Islam*, and it is offensive to speak of an Islamic believer as a *Mohammedan.*
  b. The edifice on Mount St. Alban is *Washington Cathedral* or formally *the Cathedral of SS. Peter and Paul.* The National Cathedral is a misnomer, and *Washington National Cathedral* is worse.
  c. The words *Episcopalian* and *Congregationalist* are nouns. The adjectives are *Episcopal* and *Congregational.*
  d. Do not use *sect* as a substitute for *church, congregation* or the like; the word implies dissent and exclusivity.
  e. It is the *Seventh-day Adventist Church.*
  f. The last book of the Bible is *Revelation*, not *Revelations.*
  g. Southern Presbyterians mostly belong to the *Presbyterian Church in the United States*, not to be confused with the larger *United Presbyterian Church.*
  h. No Baptist body larger than a congregation is properly called a *church.* Regional and national Baptist organizations are usually called *conventions*, except for the American Baptist Churches.

J. SEXISM

1. Sexism—the arbitrary stereotyping of men and women and their roles in life—breeds and reinforces inequality. But some words and forms are so historically and culturally imbedded that they defy efforts to eradicate them. Moreover, awkward and self-conscious new forms can interfere with readers' comprehension. Thus the rules in this section are imperfect. What matters most is to write and edit with a sense of equality, appropriateness and dignity for both sexes.

2. Life and career roles

Avoid stereotyping careers and jobs. Do not suggest that wage-earning is always done by the man or homemaking by the woman.

NO	YES
The average worker with a wife and two children . . .	*The average family of four . . .*
Housewives are feeling the effects . . .	*Consumers are feeling the effects . . .*
Mothers were warned that the toy could . . .	*Parents were warned that the toy . . .*

3. Human portrayals

   a. Portray members of both sexes as having human strengths and weaknesses, not masculine or feminine ones. Women can be bold, logical or career-oriented; men can be gentle, immature or frightened.

   b. Avoid descriptions of women that are demanding or condescending *(scatter-brained, catty, bra-burner)*. Avoid descriptions of men that focus on ineptness around the home and dependence on women for meals and health care.

   c. Avoid descriptions and photos that concentrate on physical features, clothes and habits unless they are pertinent, and unless comparable terms would be used regardless of the subject's sex.

   d. Use parallel references to the sexes.

NO	YES
the men and the ladies	*the men and the women, the women and the men,*
man and wife	*husband and wife*

4. Names and titles

  a. As noted in B1 and B2, *Mr.*, *Mrs.* and *Miss* should be used only in obituaries, in reference to couples, in quotations and for special effect. Generally use a woman's own full name in first reference and just her last name after that. Do not use *Ms.* except in direct quotations, in discussing the term itself or for special effect.

  b. When a story mentions two or more members of a family, rephrase sentences or repeat first names as needed to avoid confusion.

  c. On those rare occasions when a woman's own first name cannot be learned, use *Mrs.* and her husband's first name.

  d. Refer to a woman by her preferred name, whether it is her original name or her married name. This is especially common among performers (*Elizabeth Taylor*) and professional women (*Carolyn Agger*, wife of former Justice Abe Fortas).

5. Marital and family status and age

  a. Do not report marital status unless it is pertinent and unless its use would apply to both men and women.

  b. Refer to a divorced woman by her own first name; if it cannot be learned, use *Mrs.* and her ex-husband's name, but make clear that they are no longer married.

   Helen White, former wife of . . . ; the former Mrs. John Black; the former wife of Sen. John Black

  c. Mention or omit family relationships on the same basis for both sexes.

  d. Mention age only when germane and then on the same basis for men and women.

6. Occupations and titles

  a. In referring to particular individuals, use commonly accepted occupational titles and role descriptions.

Assemblyman John Black, Assemblywoman Mary White

b. In referring to roles in general or groups of people, use a gender-free term unless it would be awkward or artificial to do so.

TRADITIONAL	ALTERNATIVE
businessman	*business executive, business manager*
cameraman	*photographer*
college boys or *coeds*	*students*
congressman	*member of Congress, representative, legislator*
councilman	*council member*
fireman	*firefighter*
foreman	*supervisor*
ice cream man	*ice cream vendor*
mailman	*mail carrier, letter carrier*
newsman	*reporter, journalist*
policeman or *policewoman*	*police officer*
salesman	*sales clerk, salesperson*
steward or *stewardess*	*flight attendant*

c. Where no gender-free term has achieved wide acceptance, use terms that accurately identify the person's sex unless they are awkward or artificial.

Democratic chairman Robert Strauss, Republican chairwoman Mary Louise Smith; department spokeswoman

d. Where neither a gender-free term nor a feminine counterpart is in common use, traditional terms should be used even though not literally accurate.
Yeoman 1C Joan Jones; telephone lineman Joan Jones; first baseman Joan Jones

e. Most forms using *-one*, *-person* and *-people (chair-one, chairperson, chairpeople)* are awkward and hence unacceptable unless a known, formal title.

f. In reference to humanity in general, gender-free terms can frequently be used. But traditional forms are in many cases more appropriate.

TRADITIONAL	ALTERNATIVE
average man, common man	*average person*
best man for the job	*best person for the job*
man or mankind	*humanity, humans, the human race*
manhood	*adulthood*
man-in-the-street	*average citizen, ordinary voter*
manmade	*synthetic, manufactured*
primitive man	*primitive people*
workingman	*worker, work force*

g. Do not use gender-qualifiers with an occupational title unless the person's sex is pertinent. (Make it *lawyer*, not *woman lawyer*, and *nurse*, not *male nurse*.)

h. Avoid feminine variants (*poetess*) unless they are in such common use as to be part of the language. (A woman is an *alumnus, aviator, executor, Jew, poet* and *sculptor*—but an *actress, countess, masseuse, Rockette, suffragette* and *waitress*.)

PUTTING PEOPLE INTO PIGEONHOLES

By Richard Harwood

The habit of thinking in terms of stereotypes, of equating the labels we put on people with the people themselves, is a bad business. To be a "Jew" in Germany in the 1930s and 1940s was to be a "criminal." The women and children killed at Mylai were not "people," Lt. William Calley said, they were "the enemy." A policeman, the Black Panther newspaper used to remind us, is not a "person" but a "pig."

People in the news business are supposed to be conscious of these problems, to be aware of stereotypes and of what they can do to people's minds. We no longer use words like Sambo and Aunt Jemima to categorize black men and women. We no longer depict American Indians as potbellied souvenir hucksters saying "How" and "Ugh." We no longer portray Mexican Americans as peasants in Pancho Villa hats sleeping under a cactus plant. At The Post we no longer insist that the words "Red" or "Communist" should precede the word China when we are talking about China.

Nevertheless, the mass media are still full of stereotypes, labels, clichés and code words that confuse or mislead more than they inform. We wrote about "hippies" and "hard hats" as if they were scientifically delineated species of mankind. We still talk about "suburbia" and "ghettos" as if these geographical concepts had assembly-line characteristics. We still discourse on the "middle class," the "military-industrial complex," "the poor" and the "Eastern establishment" as if, like bottles of milk, they are homogenous entities. We still hang on our politicians empty labels such as "liberal," "conservative," "hawk" and "dove" as if we—and the audience out there—had some clear idea of what information these labels are intended to convey.

These habits often lead us into nothing more serious than silliness. . . . But there are times, as a British journal has noted, when "news can poison." It can poison our minds, our

Richard Harwood has been the ombudsman, assistant managing editor for national news and deputy managing editor of The Washington Post.

attitudes toward others, our perceptions of the world in which we live. The British study, carried out at the University of Leicester, found that the effect of the media in Britain on racial attitudes was to "perpetuate negative perceptions of colored people and to define the situation as one of intergroup conflict." Another effect was to create "the expectation of violence," especially among people with little firsthand knowledge of the situation.

One suspects that the same thing may be true in the United States, that in our preoccupations in the media with "white racism" on the one hand and "black militancy" on the other, we may have heightened or at least helped perpetuate "negative perceptions" and the "expectation of violence" in this country.

Robert Coles, a Harvard psychiatrist, once wrote that

some of us who are ever so clever at noticing inconsistencies in others never seem to remark upon our own confusions and mixed feelings. And all the while, I fear, we sell one another short. We categorize people, call them names like "culturally disadvantaged" or "white racists," names that say something all right, but not enough—because those declared "culturally disadvantaged" so often are at the same time shrewd, sensitive and in possession of their own culture, their own way of giving order to this world's complexities, just as those called "white racists" have other sides to themselves, can be generous and decent, can take note of and be responsive to the black man's situation.

The label is not the animal and we in the news business ought to know that by now, and know, too, that the labels and stereotypes we deal in—wittingly or not—are often more disturbing and confusing to the audience out there than the people and conditions we hang them on. We ought to know, also, that stereotypes are created not only by the repetition of a word—"hippie" or "hard hat"—but by the selection of the facts we choose to emphasize. If we decide that the only "newsworthy" facts about black people are facts about crime, public welfare and revolutionary rhetoric, we create a stereotype and deny the diversity of 20 million people.

Newspapers can do better than that. They can use language with more precision. They can develop better definitions of "news." They can recognize diversity. They can stop presenting random—and often bizarre—opinions as The Voice of The People. Above all, they can ignore the labels and stereotypes that are hung on people and things and seek out the reality of the human condition.

"Good language alone," Stuart Chase has written, "will not save mankind. But seeing the things behind the names will help us to understand the structure of the world we live in. Good language will help us to communicate with one another about the realities of our environment, where we now speak darkly, in alien tongues."

—From a News Business column in
The Washington Post, March 18, 1971

GOOD WRITING AND CORRECT USAGE

In general: Professional reporters and editors must be able to write in clear, grammatical English. This section touches on a few elements of good writing and proper usage. For those who need the additional help, many basic books and courses are available. And even the most polished writer or skillful editor can profit from an occasional hour with the works of, say, Strunk or Fowler. A list of volumes on usage appears at the end of this chapter.

A. READABILITY

Newspaper stories must be readable. They are not meant to stand as literature for the ages; they are meant to impart information to a broad readership whose education, vocabulary and comprehension vary greatly. A story about welfare reform is of little use if it is understood only by the welfare administrator and not by the welfare recipient.

1. Don't be too formal. Write in easy, conversational language. Use short sentences—perhaps a separate one for each thought. Notice the difference in these two versions.

NO	YES
The hearing, which began yesterday, is the first step toward possible revision of the 22½ percent oil depletion allowance, which oil companies consider essential to exploration and the development of reserves but which critics call an unconscionable tax giveaway.	*The hearing began yesterday. It is the first step toward possible revision of the 22½ percent oil depletion allowance. Oil companies consider the allowance essential to exploration and the development of reserves. Critics call it an unconscionable tax giveaway.*

2. Organize the story in your mind before you start to write. The traditional "five w's"—who, what, when, where and why—need not be in the lead but should be high up in the story. Most news stories can follow this rough formula:

a. A lead paragraph and two or three additional paragraphs outlining the high points of the story.

b. One or two "so what?" paragraphs explaining the story's background and significance.

    c. Elaboration, either chronologically or in descending order of importance.

3. Keep in mind these principles and examples from *The Elements of Style* by William Strunk Jr. and E. B. White: Use the active voice; use the positive form; use concrete language; emphasize nouns and verbs rather than adjectives and adverbs.

NO	YES
There were a great number of dead leaves lying on the ground.	*Dead leaves covered the ground.*
He was not very often on time.	*He usually came late.*
A period of unfavorable weather set in.	*It rained every day for a week.*

4. Avoid gobbledygook and faddish words as much as possible. When a new word or technical term must be used, put it in quotation marks if appropriate and define it at the first chance.

B. CARELESS GRAMMAR

Careless grammar contributes to bad writing. Among common errors:

1. Wrong verb tense (tense depends on the intended meaning, as in these correct examples):

    He said he was cold. (He was so at the time.)

    He said Michigan is cold in the winter. (That is the normal condition.)

    He said he had been skiing. (Past perfect tense is used because he had returned.)

    He said he was skiing on Thanksgiving. (No need to use past perfect because time is specified.)

2. Incorrect use of singular and plural:

   a. A collective noun (*couple, pair, majority, board, team, gang, herd*, etc.) may take either singular or plural construction, depending on whether it is used in a singular or plural sense. But avoid awkward phrasing and use common sense.

   > *The first couple was applauded. The couple made their appearance dressed as George and Martha Washington.* (But instead of saying *the team could not take its wives* or *their wives*, rephrase the sentence.)

   b. *Number* can be either singular or plural; when used with *the*, it is generally singular but when used with *a*, it is generally plural.

   > *A large number of accidents were reported. . . . The large number of accidents was attributed. . . .*

   c. *No one* is singular but *none* can be singular or plural, depending on sense.

   > *No one was hurt. None of the bread is fresh. None of the eggs are fresh.*

   d. *Everyone, everybody, anyone* and *anybody* take a singular verb and pronoun.

   > *Everyone takes off his coat.*

   e. *Data* requires a singular verb but similar Latin forms require a plural one.

   > *Data is gathered. The media are powerful.*

   f. Words ending in *ics* are singular or plural depending on the sense in which they are used.

   > *Politics is my job; their politics are dirty.*
   > *Tactics is an art; his tactics were subtle.*

   g. In using *or* and *nor*, the verb should agree with the nearer subject.

   > *Either he or they are going. Neither they nor he is going.*

3. Careless construction:

a. Infinitives and compounds may be split to clarify meaning and avoid ambiguity or awkwardness. (No stylebook can be definitive; Fowler has five pages on adverb placement alone.)

> *to mortally wound, hoped to at least double production, is virtually completed*

b. *Not* should be used with care; using it in the wrong place can change meaning significantly.

> *Not all boys are bad* (but some are). *All boys are not bad* (none are).

c. *Only, just* and similar qualifiers should be used next to the word they modify.

> *He spoke to only one person* (and no one else). *He only spoke to one person* (and did nothing else regarding him). *Only he* (and no one else) *spoke to one person.*

d. Time elements should follow the verb as closely as possible, but may precede it to avoid awkward construction.

> *President Black spoke to the nation yesterday. President Black yesterday described last week's defeat of his omnibus health legislation as tragic.*

e. Construction should be parallel.

NO	YES
He told me either to pay or return it.	*He told me to either pay or return it.*
Police found blood on the floor, bed and in the sink.	*Police found blood on the floor, on the bed and in the sink.*

4. Unclear references:

a. Avoid the dangling phrase.

> *Wearing only underwear and sandals, his answer brought a smile to the sheriff's face.*

b. Avoid the nonspecific pronoun.
The gunman was killed by the policeman after he allegedly hit him with a tire iron.

5. Misuse of *either/or* and *neither/nor:* Both forms should generally apply to only two elements (*either by car or by bus,* not *either by car, by bus or by train*). See Fowler for a detailed discussion.

C. SLOPPY AND LAZY WRITING

Much bad writing is the result of mere laziness or sloppiness. Among the hazards are:

1. Jargon:
budget-wise, finalize, gubernatorial mansion

2. Redundancies and extraneous words (although sometimes useful for emphasis or clarity):
advance *planning, 2:30 p.m. yesterday* afternoon, *protest* against, *were* as follows, *remanded* back, *weather* conditions, definite *decision, burn* down, free *gift,* free *pass,* general *consensus,* in order *to,* invited *guest, joined* together, mass *media,* mid-air *collision,* new *record, all* of the *people,* old *adage,* held on *Tuesday, mining* operations, *whether* or not, outer *space,* personal *friend,* proposed *plan, for recreation* purposes, qualified *expert,* quality *merchandise, high* rate of *speed, grocery* store, *strangled* to death, *filled* to capacity, *rose* to his feet, true *facts, beat* up, *reason* why

3. Stiltedness:
regarding (about), *following* (after), *prior to* (before), *accommodate* (contain), *in spite of the fact* (despite), *died of drowning* (drowned), *represents* (is), *the present time* (now), *voiced objections* (objected), *reiterate* (repeat)

4. Clichés and overworked words:
   scratched the surface, tantamount to election, limped into port, snail's pace, oil-rich, probe, quiz, sift, crisis, slate, unveil, thrust, upcoming
5. Lazy and lifeless words:
   take place, result from
6. Awkward and graceless usage:
   try and get, suicide try, shot and killed (shot to death), *have a leg amputated, ex-prime minister, shotgunned, hosted, funded, authored*
7. Nonstandard or manufactured words:
   deniability, irregardless, simplicism
8. Non sequiturs (avoid them by rephrasing):
   Educated at Yale, he ran for governor in 1960.
9. Doubtful quotes:
   "Father once spoke of having had an argument with the butcher," the defendant's 8-year-old daughter said.
10. Misuse of prepositions:

NO	YES
at the forefront	*in the forefront*
despaired about	*despaired of*
in a greater degree	*to a greater degree*
cut about the head	*cut on the head*

D. IMPRECISE USE OF WORDS

Imprecise use of words also contributes to bad writing.

1. In attribution, use *said* unless you really mean *stated, revealed, disclosed, asserted, claimed, observed, pointed out, declared, argued, continued, added, commented* and so on. Each term has a specific meaning and should not be used merely for variety.
2. Be certain of the exact meaning of words. *Burgeon*

means to sprout as well as to flourish; *fulsome* means offensive as well as excessive; *masterful* means domineering as well as masterly; *noisome* means noxious, not noisy; *prodigal* means extravagant, not remorseful.

3. Use comparatives and superlatives with care. Be certain that something really is the *best, biggest, first, heaviest* or *oldest* before saying so.

4. Pay attention to shades of meaning. For example, in writing about welfare, distinguish among *applicants, cases, claimants, individuals, families* and *recipients*—particularly when dealing with statistics.

5. Do not misuse nouns for adjectives, especially in referring to foreign countries. It is not *Iran oil situation,* but *Iranian oil situation*; not *Cyprus elections,* but *Cypriot elections.* Some leeway is permissible in headlines, however. The *U.S. Government Printing Office Style Manual* lists the correct adjectives to use in referring to foreign nations, as well as the correct nouns to use in referring to their citizens.

E. SOUND-ALIKE WORDS AND OTHER HAZARDS

The English language is a minefield of other hazards— words that sound alike, delicate nuances, shifting meanings and the like. The following examples are only a few among thousands that could be mentioned, but they serve to warn the writer and editor to be certain that the word and form used mean what is intended.

A is used before words beginning with a sounded **h** such as **hotel** and **historic**; **an** is used before words beginning with an unsounded **h** such as **honor** and **heir. A** also is used before words beginning with vowels that are sounded like consonants (**union**).

Use **about** or **approximately** for estimated figures but not **some**. Don't use both **about** and **estimated (estimated at about 5,000).** Don't use **an estimated 5,000.**

Acetic (acid); **ascetic** (austere); **esthetic** (artistic).

Act. See **Bill.**

Adultery is committed when at least one partner is married. Otherwise it is **fornication**. Animals **copulate**.

Adverse (unfavorable); **averse** (opposed).

Affect is a verb meaning to influence; **effect** as a verb means to bring about **(effect a change)** and as a noun means result.

Afraid, scared and **frightened** indicate alarm over a specific danger; **fear** and **fearful** indicate a general apprehension; **terrified** and **aghast** indicate paralysis of action.

Aggravate. See **Irritate.**

Aghast. See **Afraid.**

Aid (to assist); **aide** (assistant).

All ready (prepared); **already** (previously).

All together (grouped); **altogether** (thoroughly).

Allusion (indirect reference); **illusion** (false impression). Someone or something that is identified is not **alluded to**, but **referred to.**

An **amateur** is a nonprofessional; a **dilettante** is a dabbler; a **novice** is a beginner.

Among. See **Between.**

Amount refers to an aggregate (large amount of money); **number** refers to separate units (large number of dollar bills).

Anticipate means to foresee something; **expect**, usually the more appropriate verb, means to foresee with considerable certainty.

Any one (any single person or thing); **anyone** (any person at all).

Any way (in any manner); **anyway** (in any event).

Anxious implies desire mixed with uncertainty or worry; **eager** implies enthusiasm and impatience; **avid** implies intense desire or insatiability.

Appraise (to set a monetary value on); **apprise** (to inform).

Apt suggests possibility; **likely** suggests probability.

As. See **Because** and **Like.**

Ascent (climb); **assent** (agreement).

It's **Asian flu**, not **Asiatic flu.**

An **assassin** is someone who kills a public figure, particularly out of fanaticism or for reward; use **would-be assassin** if he made an attempt but failed.

Although both words mean to take for granted without proof, **assume** suggests the posing of a hypothesis while **presume** suggests belief that something is true.

Assure. See **Ensure.**

Audience. See **Spectator.**

Auger (tool for boring); **augur** (to be an omen of).

Avid. See **Anxious.**

One feels **bad**, not **badly** (as regards personal condition or attitude).

Baloney (nonsense); **bologna** (meat).

Ban and **bar** both refer to a legal obstacle to action. **Bar** is used in connection with the application of statutes of limitations. **Prohibit** is a more generalized and usually more appropriate verb.

Banks and **savings and loan institutions** are not the same. Be sure you know which you mean. Banks can offer checking accounts and a variety of loans; in most states and the District of Columbia, S&Ls cannot offer checking accounts and are restricted generally to mortgage loans.

Bazaar (marketplace); **bizarre** (odd).

Because indicates a direct causal relationship. **Since** and **as** explain a relationship. **Inasmuch as** means in view of the fact that. **Insofar as** means to the degree that. **Due to** usually should not be used to mean because, but when it is so used it follows a form of the verb to be and must govern a noun. (WRONG: He resigned due to ill health. RIGHT: His resignation was due to ill health.)

Behalf. On behalf of means as the formal agent or representative of; **in behalf of** means in informal support of.

Belittle means to disparage or depreciate, not merely to ridicule.

Beside (at the side); **besides** (in addition).

Better applies to one of two items; **best** applies to more than two.

One chooses (or distinguishes or stands) **between** two objects, but **among** three or more. (**Between** may be used when referring to three or more elements if each relates to the other, as in **a treaty between four nations**.)

Bi means every two (biweekly); **semi** means half (semi-monthly).

Biannual (twice a year); **biennial** (once in two years).

Proposed legislation is a **bill**; after enactment it is a **law** or an **act**. Use the subjunctive in referring to the potential effect of a bill; it **would prohibit**, not **will prohibit**.

Blame as a verb may take either **for** or **on**; John is **blamed for** the defeat; the defeat is **blamed on** John.

A **boat** is generally a small, open vessel propelled by oars, paddles, sails or small motor; anything larger is called a **ship** or **vessel** (unless it has a specialized name such as **tanker, freighter, submarine** or **ore carrier**).

Bomb. See **Canister.**

Bouillon (soup); **bullion** (gold or silver in ingots).

Bovine. See **Canine.**

Brahman (Hindu caste, breed of cattle); **brahmin** (blueblood).

Breach (break); **breech** (bottom or rear); **broach** (to make a hole, to start a discussion).

Breathe (to take a **breath**).

Bring refers to motion toward the speaker, writer or reader; **take** refers to motion away from him. The victim is **taken** to the hospital, not **brought** to it.

Broach. See **Breach.**

Burglary. See **Theft.**

Bury. See **Die.**

Bus, buses, bused, busing (referring to the vehicle); **buss, busses, bussed, bussing** (referring to a kiss).

Calendar (list of dates); **calender** (pressing machine); **colander** (strainer).

Calk (cleat); **caulk** (to make watertight).

Callous (unfeeling); **callus** (hardened skin).

Can and **could** imply capability; **may** and **might** imply permission or possibility.

Canine, feline and **bovine** are nouns as well as adjectives.

Riot squads use tear gas **canisters** or tear gas **shells**, not tear gas **bombs**; the word **bomb** refers to an explosive charge.

Canvas (cloth); **canvass** (to examine or solicit).

Capital (a city that is a seat of government); **capitol** (a legislature's building).

Carat (unit of weight for gems); **caret** (mark used by writers); **karat** (unit of fineness of gold).

Careen (to move rapidly and uncontrollably, especially nautically); **career** (to move at full speed); **carom** (to glance off).

Carousal (drunken revel); **carousel** (merry-go-round).

Cartridge. See **Rifle.**

Casket. See **Die.**

Caster (wheel for movable furniture); **castor** (perfume ingredient); **castor oil** (laxative).

Cause. See **Responsible.**

Cement is just one ingredient of **concrete**; cement holds together the concrete used in a sidewalk.

Chord (a musical term); **cord** (string or rope; anatomical part).

A **citizen** is a member of a sovereign state and shares in political rights; a **subject** owes allegiance to a monarch and often does not share in political rights; a **national** owes allegiance to a nation but need not be a citizen or even live there; Americans are technically **citizens** of their states but should be referred to as **residents** of them and their counties, cities, etc.

Class labels—**lower class**, **blue-collar**, **working class**, **middle class**, **upper class**—should be used with care.

Classic means model in nature or conforming to a recognized standard of acceptance or excellence. **Classical** refers to serious musical compositions (as opposed to those of a popular nature) and to certain historical periods, in particular the ages of ancient Greece and Rome.

Climactic (pertaining to a climax); **climatic** (pertaining to climate).

Coffin. See **Die.**

Collaborate, **collude**, **connive**, **conspire** and **scheme** have similar meanings but shades of distinction: **to**

collaborate means to work together, usually openly; **to collude** means to cooperate secretly for a deceitful purpose; **to connive** means to wink at or provide secret indulgence or assistance; **to conspire** means to plot with others to commit an illegal act; **to scheme** means to plot or to devise a plan.

A **collision** does not require two moving objects; a car can collide with a tree and waves can collide with rocks. The neutral phrasing is **Car A and Car B collided**; to say **A collided with B** suggests blame.

Collude. See **Collaborate.**

A professional entertainer gives a **comic** performance, but anyone can unwittingly give a **comical** one in trying to do something for which he is ill-suited.

To compare to is to stress similarities; **to compare with** is to take both similarities and dissimilarities into account, with emphasis usually on the latter.

Complacent (satisfied); **complaisant** (obliging).

A person is **dark-complexioned**, not **dark-complected.**

Complement (that which completes); **compliment** (praise).

Comprise means to contain or include, as in **the alphabet comprises 26 letters**; its use to mean **constitute** as in **26 letters comprise the alphabet** is considered loose; it is not correct to say **the alphabet is comprised of 26 letters.**

Concerned about (preoccupied); **concerned with** (engaged in).

Concrete. See **Cement.**

Connive and **Conspire.** See **Collaborate.**

Consul (diplomatic official); **council** (deliberative body); **counsel** (advice; a legal adviser).

Continual (repeated); **continuous** (uninterrupted).

Convince means to win over by argument; **persuade**

means to win over by appeal to reason or emotions.

Copulate. See **Adultery.**

Corespondent (person accused with the defendant); **correspondent** (one who writes).

Council and **Counsel.** See **Consul.**

Councilor (member of a council); **counselor** (adviser; lawyer; embassy aide).

Couple. See **Pair.**

Credible (believable); **creditable** (worthy of approval).

Crochet (to do fancy knitting); **crotchet** (an odd fancy).

Croquet (a lawn game); **croquette** (meat patty).

Cue (signal; billiard stick); **queue** (lineup; pigtail).

Current. See **Present.**

Use **cut in two** instead of **cut in half** unless something was really cut into two halves.

Dais. See **Podium.**

Something cannot be **partially destroyed** or **completely destroyed**; it is either **damaged** or **destroyed**.

People who cannot hear and/or talk are **deaf, mute**, or **deaf and mute**, but not **deaf mutes** or **deaf and dumb**.

Decimate originally meant to eliminate one in 10, but in current usage it means to destroy a great number or proportion.

Deprecate (disapprove of); **depreciate** (belittle; devalue). Often employed in the reflexive forms **self-deprecate** and **self-depreciate**, frequently confused. Examples of correct usage are: **The editorial deprecated the slowness of the trial; The victim was a mild-mannered, self-depreciating individual.**

Device (a scheme or contrivance); **devise** (to contrive).

Doctors **diagnose** a patient's condition, not the patient himself.

A man **dies** and is **buried** in a **coffin** by an **undertaker** or

funeral director; he does not **pass away** and is not **interred** in a **casket** by **a mortician**.

Different from is preferred although **different than** is also correct.

A **dilemma** is not simply a distasteful situation, but one entailing two unsatisfactory alternatives.

Dilettante. See **Amateur.**

Dinghy (a boat); **dingy** (drab).

Disburse (pay out); **disperse** (scatter).

Disc (phonograph record); **disk** (round, flat object).

Discomfit (to thwart, upset); **discomfort** (to make uncomfortable).

Disinterested (neutral); **uninterested** (not interested).

Dispatch. See **Haste.**

A candidate **disputes** or **rebuts** an opponent's arguments; he **refutes** them only if he disproves them.

Domicile. See **Home.**

Drier (less moist); **dryer** (device for drying articles).

One is **drunk**, but is accused of either **drunken driving** or **driving while drunk.**

Due. See **Because.**

Dumb. See **Deaf.**

During. See **While.**

Eager. See **Anxious.**

Earn. See **Paid.**

Effect. See **Affect.**

Electric generally means operated by electricity (electric clock); **electrical** means pertaining to electricity (electrical engineer); **electronic** means having the flow of electrons controlled by vacuum tubes, transistors and the like, as in a television set.

Emigrant (one who leaves a country to reside elsewhere); **immigrant** (one who enters a country for permanent residence).

Eminent (prominent); **imminent** (at hand).

Airplanes, ships and rockets have **engines** (machines for converting energy into force or motion); **motors** are small, compact engines (often electrical ones) that propel or operate cars, small vehicles and boats, appliances and the like. Both terms are used in the case of automobiles.

Enormity (immoderation, outrageousness); **enormousness** (great size).

Ensure (to make an outcome inevitable); **insure** (to provide insurance); **assure** (remove worry or uncertainty). Events are **ensured**; objects or lives are **insured**; persons are **assured**.

Entitled(deserving of); **titled** (named).

Entomology (study of insects); **etymology** (study of the derivation of words).

Envelop (to surround); **envelope** (container).

Epitome is the embodiment or ideal representation of something, not a high point or climax; one's attire may be the **epitome** of fashion, but a triumph is not the **epitome** of a career.

Euphemism (pleasant name for an unpleasant thing); **euphuism** (artificially elegant literary style).

Expatiate (to elaborate); **expiate** (to atone for).

Expect. See **Anticipate.**

Expedite. See **Haste.**

Faker (fraud); **fakir** (holy man).

Farther (at a greater distance); **further** (to a greater degree).

Faze (bother); **phase** (a stage).

Fear. See **Afraid.**

Feline. See **Canine.**

Write **fewer than 60** attended, not **less than 60** or **under 60**; **less** refers to size rather than to number, and **under** refers to direction.

Final (last); **finale** (concluding part).

Fine. See **Sentence.**

Flack (press agent); **flak** (antiaircraft shells).

Flagrant (glaringly evident); **fragrant** (having a pleasing smell).

Flammable, inflammable; inflammation; inflammatory. The first two terms are synonomous, but use **flammable** because it is shorter and not subject to misinterpretation. The other two words have nothing to do with fire. **Inflammation** is principally a medical term, while **inflammatory** has to do with the arousal of emotions.

Flaunt (to display boastfully); **flout** (to treat with disdain).

Flounder (to struggle clumsily); **founder** (to become disabled, to sink).

Forbear (refrain); **forebear** (ancestor).

Forbid. See **Prohibit.**

Forbidding (menacing, difficult); **foreboding** (a prediction or portent).

Forego (precede); **forgo** (abstain from).

Fornication. See **Adultery.**

Fortuitous (happening by chance); **fortunate** (lucky).

Frightened. See **Afraid.**

Funeral director. See **Die.**

Further. See **Farther.**

Gamut (the full extent); **gantlet** (a flogging ordeal); **gauntlet** (a glove).

Gangster. See **Theft.**

Gibe (taunt); **jibe** (conform, shift course).

Glacier (ice field); **glazier** (one who puts glass in windows).

Glutinous (like glue); **gluttonous** (eating immoderately).

Gothic is capitalized except when used to mean fantastic or gloomy, as in a **gothic** novel.

Got is preferred to **gotten.**

Gourmand (hearty eater); **gourmet** (connoisseur of food).

A college **graduates** a class; the student either **graduates from** college or **is graduated** by a college, but he does not **graduate college.**

Grisly (gruesome); **gristly** (containing gristle); **grizzled** (streaked with gray); **grizzly** (bear).

Gunman. See **Theft.**

Hail (to greet); **hale** (take into court; healthy).

Flags generally fly at **half-staff**; ships and naval shore installations fly them at **half-mast.** Flags are lowered, not raised, to half-mast or half-staff.

Hangar (shelter for aircraft); **hanger** (that from which articles hang).

Hanged (by the neck until dead); **hung** (as a picture).

Happen. See **Occur.**

Hardly and **scarcely** are in effect negatives, and the rule against double-negative construction applies to them (**he can hardly**, not **he can't hardly**).

Haste implies careless rapidity; **hurry** implies impetuous rapidity; **dispatch** and **expedite** imply efficient rapidity; **speed** implies controlled rapidity.

Healthful (conducive to health); **healthy** (possessing health).

Heart failure is involved in every death. Be specific. A person dies after a **heart attack** or dies of **heart disease** or suffers from a **heart condition** or a **heart ailment.**

Helix. See **Spiral.**

High. See **Tall.**

Hippy (large-hipped); **hippie** (flower child).

Historic means history-making, significant in history or important because of age. **Historical** means pertaining to history.

Hoard (to save; what is saved); **horde** (a multitude).

Holdup man. See **Theft.**

A **holocaust** kills many people or causes great destruction; it is not just a bad fire.

A person lives in his **home**, which may be a **house** or an **apartment** or some other type of dwelling; **residence** and **domicile** refer to the place where a person legally resides.

Hopefully is correctly used when it means full of hope and is correctly linked to the subject and verb. **(The farmer looked forward to the harvest hopefully.)** It is frequently incorrectly used, however, as a "dangling" adverb to mean it is hoped that or let us hope. **(Hopefully, the weather will change.)**

Horde. See **Hoard.**

Hurry. See **Haste.**

Idle (not busy); **idol** (image of a god); **idyll** (poem; carefree episode).

Immigrant. See **Emigrant.**

Imminent. See **Eminent.**

To imply is to indicate or convey some idea without specifically stating it. **To infer** is to conclude or deduce an idea that has not been specifically stated.

Inapt (inappropriate); **inept** (incompetent).

Inasmuch and **Insofar.** See **Because.**

Do not say **the six include** if all six are named; say **the six are.**

Indecent. See **Vulgar.**

Indict (to charge with a crime); **indite** (to put into writing).

Infer. See **Imply.**

It is **to infringe**, not **to infringe on**, a right or privilege. **(Brown infringed Black's patent.)**

Ingenious (clever); **ingenuous** (lacking guile).

Inherent; innate; intrinsic. The three mean virtually the same thing, but there is an element of passivity in **innate** and an element of necessity in **intrinsic. (The motor has an inherent defect. Cattle are innately stupid. A free press is intrinsic to the democratic system.)**

Inhibit (hinder); **prohibit** (forbid).

Injuries are **received** or **inflicted**, not **suffered** or **sustained.**

Insidious (cunning); **invidious** (provoking discontent or envy).

Insure. See Ensure.

Inter. See Die.

Irritate means to annoy, bother or make sore or inflamed; **aggravate** means to make worse or more severe.

Jibe. See Gibe.

Karat. See Carat.

A nautical **knot** equals 6,076.10 feet an hour or 1.15 miles an hour; a ship sails at 4 knots, not 4 knots an hour.

Aircraft make all kinds of **landings**; distinguish among an **emergency** landing (when safety is seriously threatened), a **precautionary** landing (to investigate and correct mechanical trouble) and an **unscheduled** landing for delivery of a baby.

Landlord and **slumlord** have derogatory connotations; use **building owner** instead.

Law. See Bill.

Lay and **lie** are especially troublesome. The correct forms:

> **lay (a transitive verb, taking an object)—I lay the book down, I laid, I am laying, I have laid, I had laid, I will lay, he lays; lie (intransitive, taking no object)—I lie, I lay, I am lying, I had lain, I have lain, I will lie, he lies.**

Lectern. See **Podium.**

Lend. See **Loan.**

Less. See **Fewer.**

Liable refers to a legal obligation or exposure (**liable** to a $500 fine); **subject** implies continuing liability or likelihood (**subject** to periods of depression); **susceptible** implies predisposition, naivete, lack of resistance (**susceptible** to a salesman's pitch).

Lightening (making less heavy); **lightning** (electrical discharge).

Like, as, as if and **as though** present problems. Changing standards and the words' many functions make rule setting hazardous. But in general:

Like and **as** cause little difficulty as prepositions. **Like** suggests resemblance or contrast and **as** suggests degree or correlation.

> **Just like his father; no place like home.**
> **Fit as a fiddle; as good as gold.**

Like should seldom be used as a conjunction in place of **as, as if** or **as though.**

> **Bread prices will not become prohibitive as** (not **like**) **meat prices did.**
> **He lay there as if** (not **like**) **he were dead.**

Bernstein offers this rule of thumb: **as** is usually correct if the introduced element has a verb; **like** is usually correct if it does not.

> **He ran as he had never run before; he ran like the wind.**
> **Winston tastes good as a cigarette should; Winston tastes like a cigarette.**

Likely is both an adjective (a **likely** candidate) and an adverb (it will **likely** rain). Also see **Apt.**

Linage (lines of advertising); **lineage** (ancestry).

Lineament (facial contour); **liniment** (healing solution).

Loan can be used as a verb, but **lend** is preferred; you

Loan can be used as a verb, but **lend** is preferred; you lend your friend money and he repays the **loan**. The past tense of **lend** is **lent**.

Loath (reluctant); **loathe** (to detest).

Local (close by); **locale** (site).

A building is **located** somewhere; use **situated** only to refer to a commanding or significant site (**situated** on a hill).

Luxuriant (lush, flourishing); **luxurious** (elegant, sumptuous).

Mach refers to the speed of sound; **Mach 2** means twice the speed of sound (which is 750 mph at sea level and 660 mph at 30,000 feet).

A **majority** is more than half; a **plurality** is the highest number but not necessarily a majority or a winning margin.

Manikin (a model of the human body with detachable parts); **mannequin** (a live clothes model or a clothes display dummy).

Manner (behavior); **manor** (estate). (An aristocrat is to the **manor** born.)

Mantel (shelf); **mantle** (cloak).

Marital (pertaining to marriage); **martial** (pertaining to war).

Material (stuff of which something is made); **materiel** (military supplies).

May, might. See **Can, could.**

May Day (spring festival, international labor holiday); **Mayday** (distress signal).

Use **meanwhile** or **in the meantime,** but not **meantime** or **in the meanwhile.**

Men are **men** and **women** are **women;** generally avoid **males** and **females.** And not all **women** are **ladies,** and not all **men** are **gentlemen.**

A **metaphor is a figure of speech in which a similarity is implied (Ken is a bulldog).** A **simile** is a figure of speech in which a similarity is expressly stated **(Scott is like a bulldog).**

Meteoroids are particles that fly around in space; **meteors** are meteoroids that enter earth's atmosphere, often producing a fiery streak (shooting star); **meteorites** are meteors that survive the flight and land on earth as a mass of stone or metal.

Mobster. See **Theft.**

Mold (fungus, form for shaping); **molt** (to shed).

Write **more than 60** attended, not **over 60; over** refers to physical location.

Mortician. See **Die.**

Motor. See **Engine.**

Mucus (noun: secreted liquid); **mucous** (adjective: giving off mucus).

Mute. See **Deaf.**

Mutual (shared); **reciprocal** (interacting).

National. See **Citizen.**

Nauseated (past tense of verb to nauseate); **nauseous** (causing or affected by nausea).

Nickel (metal); **nickle** (coin).

When a prosecutor or plaintiff discontinues a case by entering a **nolle prosequi,** the noun is **nol pros** and the verbs are **nol-pros, nol-prosses** and **nol-prossed.**

Not only . . . but also. As a matter of grammatical balance, the adverb **also**—or an equivalent like **too** or **as well**—is required to complement the adverb **only,** except when the second element does not parallel the first one, but intensifies it. **He purchased not only a pistol, but also a rifle. The man is not only a bully, but a vicious, unprincipled individual.**

Novice. See **Amateur.**

Number. See **Amount.**

Obscene. See **Vulgar.**

Accidents and other unexpected events **occur** or **happen**; planned events **take place.**

Odious (hateful); **odorous** (fragrant).

Oh is used to express emotion in everyday situations and is separated by a comma from another word used in conjunction with it **(Oh, help me!).** **O** is used in solemn or poetic invocations and is not followed by a comma **(O Caesar!).**

Onto refers to movement to a position on, not merely to location on; one sets something **on** a table, but a cat climbs **onto** it. **Upon** refers to movement upward to or to being in a high position, not merely situated on.

Oral. See **Verbal.**

Ordinance (a law); **ordnance** (military weapons and ammunition).

Over. See **More.**

A person **is paid** (not **earns** or **makes**) $2 an hour.

Pair refers to two identical or matched objects that belong together or are used together (**a pair** of gloves). **Couple** refers to two objects of the same sort but not necessarily belonging together (a **couple** of pencils). A man and his wife are usually a **couple** but they may be a newlywed **pair** or a **pair** of bridge partners.

Palate (part of the mouth); **palette** (artist's paint board); **pallet** (storage box).

Parameter (a general boundary or characteristic element); **perimeter** (a closed curve bounding an area).

Part. See **Portion.**

Partly is the adverbial form of **part** and refers to a portion of a whole (**partly** luck, **partly** skill); **partially** is the adverbial form of **partial** and refers to degree or extent (**partially** blind).

Pass away. See **Die.**

Pedigreed. See **Purebred.**

Use **people** when referring to a segment of humanity; use **persons** when referring to individuals. (The **people** of Paris mourned . . . ; hundreds of **persons** attended; 27 **persons** were arrested.)

Restrict the Latin **per** to such phrases as **per capita** and **per diem**; say **miles an hour** (but abbreviate it **mph**); but sometimes **per** is preferable (monthly rent **per** room).

Be careful to distinguish between **percent** and **percentage** points; if enrollment goes up from 10 **percent** to 20 **percent**, it has risen by 10 **percentage** points but by 100 **percent**; if a president's popularity drops from 60 **percent** to 40 **percent** in a year, it has dropped by 20 **percentage** points or by $33^{1/3}$ **percent**. In such cases, it is essential to specify the raw figures.

Peremptory (decisive, absolute); **preemptory** (having prior claim).

Perimeter. See **Parameter.**

Perquisite (privilege, special benefit); **prerequisite** (requirement).

Persons. See **People.**

Perspective (view); **prospective** (expected).

Persuade. See **Convince.**

Pistol. See **Rifle.**

Plurality. See **Majority.**

A speaker stands on a **podium** or **dais** and reads his speech from a **lectern.**

Pompon (a flower or ornamental puff); **pom-pom** (antiaircraft gun).

Portion means an allotment, share or limited quantity; otherwise use **part.**

Precedence (priority); **precedent** (example for future use).

Precipitant or **precipitate** (headlong, rash); **precipitous** (steep).

Premier (ranking cabinet minister); **premiere** (first performance).

Prescribe (to order, direct); **proscribe** (to outlaw, prohibit).

The **present** is right now; the **current** time is this general period; **presently** means either in a little while (we shall go **presently**) or now (the tools **presently** at hand).

Presume. See **Assume.**

Principal (foremost; leading participant; head of a school); **principle** (rule, standard).

You **prohibit from**; you **forbid to**. Also see **Ban.**

Prophecy (noun: a prediction); **prophesy** (verb: to predict).

Proscribe. See **Prescribe.**

Prostate (male gland); **prostrate** (prone).

A **protagonist** is a leading actor or character, as well as a champion of a cause.

Provided and **providing** are both correct and mean on condition that or with the understanding that.

Pupils should be reserved for nursery and elementary school children; older children and adults are **students.**

Animals are **purebred** or **thoroughbred** (having undiluted blood lines), **standardbred** (bred to specific standards) and **pedigreed** (having a registered pedigree). Race horses are **Thoroughbreds** (flats) or **Standardbreds** (trotters) and both words are capitalized.

Quell (suppress, crush); **quench** (douse, satisfy thirst).

Rack (to trouble, torment, afflict, as to **rack** one's brain); **wrack** (to destroy, as the storm-**wracked** city).

Rank (hierarchical position); **ranking** (specific numerical classification, especially in sports and games.)

Ravaging (laying waste); **ravishing** (attractive, plundering, despoiling).

Reapportionment refers to state legislatures; **redistricting** refers to congressional districts.

Rebut. See **Dispute.**

Reciprocal. See **Mutual.**

Refinish (to give a new surface); **refurbish** (brighten or renovate).

A bill is not necessarily a tax **reform** or welfare **reform** measure just because its sponsors say so; tax **revision** is safer.

Refurbish. See **Refinish.**

Refute. See **Dispute.**

A **replica** is made by the original creator or under his supervision; a **reproduction, copy** or **duplicate** is made by others.

Residence. See **Home.**

Resident. See **Citizen.**

Respectably (deserving respect); **respectfully** (with respect); **respectively** (in turn).

Only persons or animals, not things, can bear **responsibility**; a storm **causes** death but is not **responsible** for it.

Restive (unruly, balky); **restless** (fidgety, eager for a change).

Revision. See **Reform.**

Revolver. See **Rifle.**

The **Richter scale** measures ground motion as recorded on a seismograph. The scale goes from one to 10, and every increase of one means a tenfold increase in magnitude. A quake with a reading of four can cause moderate damage; one with a reading of six, considerable damage.

A **rifle** has a rifled or helical bore that causes a bullet to spin; a **shotgun** has a smooth bore. Use **pistol** unless you know it was a **revolver** or **semiautomatic.** Rifles and pistols fire **cartridges,** which consist of a **bullet** and a **cartridge case**. Shotguns fire **shells** containing **shot**.

Robbery. See **Theft.**

A person does not **run** a business; he **manages** or **conducts** it; he might **run** a bookie operation or a clique might **run** a city, though.

The verb **sanction** can mean either to approve or to disapprove, so it is best avoided. The noun **sanction**, generally used in the plural, means a penalty.

Sanguinary (bloody, blood-thirsty); **sanguine** (blood-red, optimistic).

Savings and Loan. See **Bank.**

Scarcely. See **Hardly.**

Scared. See **Afraid.**

Scheme. See **Collaborate.**

Scot and **Scottish** are preferred; **scotch** is supposedly disliked by the Scots but is acceptable and indeed widely used (whiskey, tweed, terrier).

Sear (to burn); **seer** (a prophet); **sere** (withered).

Seasonable (appropriate to a season); **seasonal** (connected with a season). Warm weather in summer is **seasonable**, but a lifeguard's job is **seasonal**.

Semi. See **Bi.**

Sensual (carnal, worldly); **sensuous** (experienced through the senses).

One is not **sentenced to** 30 days in jail and **a $500 fine**; he is **sentenced to** 30 days in jail **and fined** $500. And instead of saying the maximum penalty is $500 **and/or** 30 days in jail, say it is a $500 **fine**, 30 days **in jail or both**.

Sewage (waste matter); **sewerage** (system of sewers).

Shell. See **Canister.**

Ship. See **Boat.**

Shotgun. See **Rifle.**

Simile. See **Metaphor.**

Since as adverb, conjunction or preposition carries the time frame to the point of writing, and so calls for use of the present perfect tense. **(Since he took the job he has lived in Chicago.)**

Situated. See **Located.**

Slumlord. See **Landlord.**

The past tense of **sneak** is **sneaked**; use **snuck** only in direct quotations.

Some. See **About.**

Space technically begins where the earth's atmosphere ends (about 1,000 miles from the surface); however, the term also applies in orbital flight to the area about 100 miles above the earth's surface; use **interplanetary, interstellar** or **intergalactic** space rather than **outer** space or **deep** space, when precision is important.

Spectators **watch** events; audiences can **listen to** or **watch** programs.

A **spiral** curve is two-dimensional, as is one drawn on a flat piece of paper; a **helix** or **helical curve** is three-dimensional, as is the rifling of a barrel. However, **spiral** is more commonly understood and is therefore acceptable in ordinary usage (a **spiral** staircase).

Stalactite (limestone column hanging from cave ceiling or wall); **stalagmite** (one rising from floor).

Stanch (to check or stop the flow of, as blood); **staunch** (steadfast).

Standardbred. See **Purebred.**

Stationary (not moving); **stationery** (writing materials).

Statue (a piece of sculpture); **stature** (physical build or height); **statute** (a law).

Steal. See **Theft.**

Steam shovels don't exist today; they are **power** shovels.

Stimulant (excitant); **stimulus** (incentive).

Students. See **Pupils.**

Subject. See **Citizen** and **Liable.**

Susceptible. See **Liable.**

Swath (mowed strip; path of a storm); **swathe** (to bandage).

Take. See **Bring.**

Take place. See **Occur.**

Tall implies dimension; **high** implies location. Thus: A **tall** man leaned from a **high** window in a **tall** building.

Tantamount (equivalent to) and **virtually** (in essence, or almost entirely) are hackneyed but acceptable.

Taunt (to tease); **taut** (stretched tight).

The relative pronoun **that** is used to introduce a restrictive clause and does not take commas. (The house **that** burned was 50 years old.) **Which** is used to introduce a nonrestrictive clause and takes commas. (The house, **which** burned, was 50 years old.)

The conjunction **that** is often unnecessary and should be eliminated where possible; but use it to avoid confusion, especially when another word comes between the verb and object. (The mayor announced today **that** the summer program will begin June 1.)

Theft and **stealing** mean taking someone's property, whether the victim is present or not; **robbery** means taking something from a person by force or threat; a **holdup** is a robbery involving a weapon; **burglary** is breaking and entering with the purpose of committing a felony.

Persons who commit such crimes are **thieves, robbers, holdup men** or **burglars.** A robber or holdup man may also be a **gunman.** But a robber is not necessarily a **bandit** (a marauding outlaw) or a **gangster** or **mobster** (a member of a gang or mob.)

Thoroughbred. See **Purebred.**

Thrash (to beat); **thresh** (to shake grain).

Timber (trees); **timbre** (quality of sound). (**Lumber** is milled timber.)

It is tinker's **dam**, not **damn**.

Titled. See **Entitled.**

Tortuous (devious; winding); **torturous** (inflicting pain).

Transient, transitory. Both mean of brief duration, but the former is applied to persons and the latter to events or situations.

A **trio** (or **quartet**) is a set of **three** (or **four**), such as a musical group; it is not a casual group of three who get together for a drive or a holdup.

Trooper (cavalryman; state policeman); **trouper** (member of a troupe, veteran actor).

Jets are powered by **turbines**; if a jet engine turns a propeller it is a **turboprop.**

Under. See **Fewer.**

Venal (corruptible, bribable); **venial** (minor, excusable).

Verbal means related to words, either written or spoken, rather than to action. It is often erroneously used to contrast with written; the correct expression of contrast is **oral** versus **written.**

Vertex (highest point); **vortex** (whirlpool).

Vessel. See **Boat.**

Vice (bad habit); **vise** (gripping tool).

Virtually. See **Tantamount.**

Vulgar means coarse; **indecent** means not conforming to moral standards; **obscene** means carnally repugnant.

Waiver (act of relinquishing); **waver** (to falter).

Which. See **That.**

While refers to a period of time, not to a moment; one is hit **while** crossing the street, but **when** stepping off a curb; **during** means throughout the course of.

In obituaries, say a man is survived by his **wife**, not by his **widow**.

Women. See **Men.**

Wrack. See **Rack.**

Written. See **Verbal.**

Yoga (the discipline); **yogi** (the adherent).

Zoom as an aviation term refers only to upward motion. A plane can **zoom** into the stratosphere, but not down toward earth, though a car can **zoom** down a road and a camera can **zoom** in on a subject.

REFERENCE BOOKS ON ENGLISH USAGE
(In order of most recent publication)

Harper Dictionary of Contemporary Usage. William Morris and Mary Morris. New York: Harper & Row, 1975.

Dictionary of Problem Words & Expressions. Harry Shaw. New York: McGraw-Hill Book Co., 1975.

The Elements of Style. William Strunk Jr. and E. B. White. Second Edition. New York: The Macmillan Co., 1972.

American Usage: The Consensus. Roy H. Copperud. New York: Van Nostrand Reinhold Co., 1970.

The American Heritage Dictionary of the English Language. William Morris, ed. Boston: Houghton Mifflin, 1969. (This is the only general dictionary that pays particular attention to usage, with capsule comments in that field scattered through its entries. These comments were prepared with the assistance of a panel of 100 writers, speakers and educators.)

Modern American Usage: A Guide. Wilson Follet, Jacques Barzun and others. New York: Grossett & Dunlap, 1966.

The Careful Writer: A Modern Guide to English Usage. Theodore M. Bernstein. New York: Atheneum, 1965.

Modern English Usage. H. W. Fowler. Second Edition,

Revised by Sir Ernest Gowers. New York: Oxford University Press, 1965.

A *Dictionary of Usage and Style.* Roy H. Copperud. New York: Hawthorn Books, 1964.

A *Dictionary of Contemporary American Usage.* Bergen Evans and Cornelia Evans. New York: Random House, 1957.

A *Dictionary of American-English Usage.* Margaret Nicholson. New York: Oxford University Press, 1957.

ABBREVIATIONS

A. *Abbreviation style*
B. *Acronyms*
C. *Dates and time*
D. *Headlines*
E. *Measurement*
F. *Places*
G. *Organizations*
H. *Ranks*
I. *Titles*
J. *Miscellany*

In general: Abbreviations are meant not only to save space but also to facilitate comprehension. Unfamiliar, unintelligible or confusing abbreviations defeat the latter purpose. And overabbreviation detracts from both clarity and typographical appearance.

A. ABBREVIATION STYLE

1. All-capitals abbreviations generally do not take periods and upper-lowercase or lowercase abbreviations generally do take periods.

CBS; Corp., c.o.d.

2. All-capitals abbreviations of places (and of the United Nations) take periods.

   L.A., N.C., U.S., U.K., U.S.S.R., U.N.

3. Upper-lowercase and lowercase abbreviations of technical measurements do not take periods when used with figures.

   100-cc capsule, 2,000 rpm

4. Freer use of abbreviations may be made in headlines and even freer use may be made in statistical and tabular matter to save space or to keep matter on one line.

B. ACRONYMS

1. Acronyms come and go; they may be reasonably well known one year and forgotten the next. At The Post, the style monitor determines when they are acceptable for use. Among abbreviations that may or may not be acceptable at any given moment are:

   GATT (General Agreement on Tariffs and Trade), *GAW* (guaranteed annual wage), *SALT* (strategic arms limitation talks), *VISTA* (Volunteers in Service to America)

2. Acronyms are capitalized unless they have become common words in their own right:

   SCORE (Service Corps of Retired Executives), *DEW* (Distant Early Warning) *Line*; but *scuba* (self-contained underwater breathing apparatus) and *laser* (light amplification by stimulated emission of radiation)

3. Be wary of using corporate or promotional acronyms. Generally capitalize only the first letter regardless of the preference of the affected organization.

   Amtrak, Amvets, Exxon, Citgo, Geico

C. DATES AND TIME

1. Five of the months are not abbreviated:
   March, April, May, June, July
2. The other seven are abbreviated in specific date usage.
   Dec. 23, 1974, or just *Dec. 23 (*but *December 1974)*
3. The correct abbreviations for those are:
   Jan., Feb., Aug., Sept., Oct., Nov., Dec.
4. Use *A.D.* and *B.C.* but *a.m.* and *p.m.* and *EST* (capitalized).

D. HEADLINES

1. Abbreviations are valuable in the writing and comprehension of headlines, but avoid overuse and unnecessary use. For example, *Klan* occupies less typespace than *KKK.*
2. Most all-capitals abbreviations are acceptable in headlines. Use periods with place names.
   *U.S., N.Y., L.A., D.C., P.G. (*for Prince George's County), *FBI, NAACP, OAS, GOP*
3. Avoid upper-lowercase abbreviations in headlines wherever possible, including abbreviations for states. Use of *Md., Mich., Calif., Pr. George's* and the like is typographically unattractive.
4. Certain abbreviations that should be avoided in stories are acceptable in headlines.
   AF, VD, JFK

E. MEASUREMENT

1. Such terms as *year, hour, mile, meter, pound* and *cent* are generally spelled out, but they may be abbreviated in statistical and tabular matter. Metric abbreviations do not take periods. Typical abbreviations (for both singular and plural forms) include:

yr., hr., min., sec.; mi., km, yd., m, ft., in., mm;
lb., oz., kg, g; sq. in., cc; ct.; tsp.; tbl.

2. Terms of technical measurement may be abbreviated without periods, but unfamiliar terms should be spelled out in first reference, followed by the abbreviation in parentheses.

65 mph, 3,000 rpm, 20 British thermal units
(Btu), 30 pounds per square inch (psi)

F. PLACES

1. Spell out *United States* as a noun; use the abbreviation *U.S.* as an adjective, in headlines and captions and when stated in a direct quotation; do not use periods in abbreviations of federal agencies or in designations of ships and roads.

the United States protested; the U.S. protest; U.S.
Protests Shelling; he said it "is high time for the
U.S. to protest"; USIA, USS Forrestal, US-40

2. Do not abbreviate names of U.S. possessions, foreign nations or Canadian provinces, even in datelines. (*U.S.S.R.* may be used sparingly, but *Soviets, Moscow* and *Russia* are better.)

3. Abbreviate the names of most states when used after the names of towns, cities, counties and physical locations such as a national park.

   a. Use the following abbreviations (not the two-letter Postal Service abbreviations):

   Ala., Ariz., Ark., Calif., Colo., Conn., D.C., Del.,
   Fla., Ga., Ill., Ind., Kan., Ky., La., Mass., Md.,
   Mich., Minn., Miss., Mo., Mont., N.C., N.D.,
   Neb., Nev., N.H., N.J., N.M., N.Y., Okla., Ore.,
   Pa., R.I., S.C., S.D., Tenn., Tex., Va., Vt., Wash.,
   Wis., W. Va., Wyo.

b. Do not abbreviate the names of these states:
Alaska, Hawaii, Idaho, Iowa, Maine, Ohio, Utah

4. Generally do not abbreviate the names of cities, counties or such places as Long Island.

a. Spell out *District of Columbia* (or *District*) as a noun; *D.C.* may be used as an adjective and as a headline or caption noun.

b. All-capitals abbreviations such as *N.Y.*, *L.A.* and *P.G.* (for Prince George's County, Md.) may be used in headlines.

5. In writing addresses:

a. Abbreviate specific addresses but spell out general locations.
lived at 2340 P St. NW, at 23rd and P streets NW, on P Street NW or in Northwest

b. The preferred abbreviations are *Ave.*, *St.*, *Blvd.*, *Cir.*, *Ct.*, *Dr.*, *Hwy.*, *La.*, *Pkwy.*, *Rd.*, *Rte.*, *Ter.*

c. Do not abbreviate *Place*, *Plaza*, *Point*, *Port* or *Oval*.

6. Do not abbreviate *fort* and *mount* except to save space in headlines.
attack on Fort Sumter, climbed Mount Whittier, mayor of Fort Worth, visit to Mount Vernon

7. Generally abbreviate saint or sainte in proper names.
St. Louis, Sault Ste. Marie (but Saint John, New Brunswick)

G. ORGANIZATIONS

1. The use of an organization's initials varies according to how recognizable they are.

a. Some initials are so well known that the name need not be spelled out unless desired for emphasis.

ABC, AFL-CIO, CARE, CBS, CIA, FBI, GOP, NAACP, NATO, NCAA, NFL, NHL, PTA, ROTC, TVA

b. Other initials are less familiar, and the name should be spelled out in first reference.

. . . according to the National Aeronautics and Space Administration. The reason, NASA said, is . . .

c. Still other initials are so unfamiliar that they should be used only to avoid excessive repetition of the full name. If used, spell out the name in first reference and enclose the initials in parentheses.

. . . according to the National Retail Dry Goods Association (NRDGA).

d. For simplicity's sake, lengthy but familiar names may be abbreviated in the lead paragraph and spelled out at the first opportunity.

School lunches will cost nearly 20 percent more next year, Assistant HEW Secretary Mary White said today. White, who heads the Health, Education and Welfare Department's . . .

e. Avoid using informal governmental and military abbreviations except in such specialized copy as the Federal Diary.

OE (Office of Education), *CINCPAC* (commander in chief, Pacific)

2. Spell out *United Nations* as a noun. Use the abbreviation *U.N.* (with periods) in headlines and as an adjective. Do not use periods with all-capitals abbreviations of U.N. bodies.

The United Nations voted . . . ; U.N. Votes to Send Aid; . . . by the U.N. Security Council; UNESCO, UNICEF

3. Generally use the abbreviations *Co., Corp., Bros., Inc.*

and *Ltd.* in full and short-form corporate names, but spell out the words in cultural usage.

> *General Motors Corp. (but Corporation for Public Broadcasting), R. H. Macy & Co., the Macy Co. (but Metropolitan Opera Company, Smothers Brothers)*

4. Spell out *association, bureau, department* and *division* in both corporate and governmental usage.

> *National Automobile Dealers Association, Justice Department, Chevrolet Division*

H. RANKS

1. Abbreviate military ranks preceding names (except those spelled out in the following lists).

   a. Army: commissioned officers—*Gen., Lt. Gen., Maj. Gen., Brig. Gen., Col., Lt. Col., Maj., Capt., 1st Lt., 2nd Lt.*; enlisted personnel—*Chief Warrant Officer, Warrant Officer, Army Sgt. Maj., Command Sgt. Maj., Staff Sgt. Maj., 1st Sgt., Master Sgt., Platoon Sgt., Sgt. 1st Class, Spec. 7, Staff Sgt., Spec. 6, Sgt., Spec. 5, Cpl., Spec. 4, Pfc., Pvt. 2, Pvt. 1.*

   b. Navy: commissioned officers—*Adm., Vice Adm., Rear Adm., Commodore, Capt., Cmdr., Lt. Cmdr., Lt., Lt. j.g., Ensign*; enlisted personnel—*Warrant Officer, Master Chief Petty Officer, Senior Chief Petty Officer, Chief Petty Officer, Petty Officer 1st Class, Petty Officer 2nd Class, Petty Officer 3rd Class, Seaman, Seaman Apprentice, Seaman Recruit, Midshipman.*

   c. Marine Corps: ranks and abbreviations for commissioned officers are the same as those in the Army; warrant officer ratings are the same as those in the Navy; other enlisted personnel—*Sgt.*

Maj., Master Gunnery Sgt., 1st Sgt., Staff Sgt., Sgt., Cpl., Lance Cpl., Pfc., Pvt.

d. Air Force: ranks and abbreviations for commissioned officers are the same as those in the Army; enlisted personnel—*Chief Master Sgt., Senior Master Sgt., Master Sgt., Tech. Sgt., Staff Sgt., Sgt., Airman 1st Class, Airman, Airman Basic.*

2. As a rule, do not continue using the rank before a name in subsequent references; use simply *Black* or *the general.* But if the rank must be used with the name in a subsequent reference, use the form *Gen. Black* instead of *Brig. Gen. Black.*

3. Spell out and capitalize *General of the Army, Fleet Admiral* and *Field Marshal* preceding a name.

4. Do not abbreviate such ratings and job descriptions as *radarman, navigator* and *machinist.*

5. Do not use periods in short-form descriptions of servicewomen *(Wacs, Waves, Wrens, Spars)* or the abbreviation *WAC* for the *Women's Army Corps.*

6. Do not use the form *Col. John Black (Ret.);* use *John Black, a retired colonel,* or *retired Army colonel John Black* instead.

7. When referring to the ranks of police officers and firefighters, use the same abbreviations that the military uses. If necessary, use a departmental or branch reference before the rank.

Fire Capt. John Black, Police Lt. John Black, Detective Sgt. Mary White

I. TITLES

1. Use the abbreviations *Gov., Lt. Gov., Sen.* and *Rep.* and their plurals preceding a name.

Gov. John Black, Govs. John Black and Mary White, Gov.-elect John Black (but former governor John Black)

2. Use the abbreviations *Dr., Prof., Fr., Msgr., the Rev.* and *the Rt. Rev.* and their plurals preceding names.
> *Dr. Mary White, Profs. John Black and Mary White, Fr. Black, Msgr. Black*

3. Abbreviate courtesy titles (but not their plurals and not protocol titles).
> *Mr. John Black, Mrs. Mary White, Mr. John Black and Mr. Peter Jones (not Messrs. John Black and Peter Jones), His Excellency John Black* and *the Honorable Mary White (not the Hon. Mary White)*

4. Do not abbreviate *attorney general, auditor general, commandant, detective, district attorney, governor general, secretary, secretary general, superintendent* or *treasurer.*

J. MISCELLANY

1. Some abbreviations have become part of the language and need not be spelled out (although the full word or phrase may make for more graceful writing).
> *AWOL, GI, IOU, MP, POW, PT boat, SOS, TB, TNT, TV*

2. Abbreviate (or use initials or short forms of):
   a. Academic and religious degrees:
   > *BA, DDS, LLD, MA, PhD, SJ*

   b. Colleges and universities:
   > *AU* (American), *GWU* (George Washington), *GU* (Georgetown), *NVCC* (Northern Virginia Community College), *U-Md., U-Va., OSU, SMU, UCLA*

   c. Names (if preferred or accepted by the individual or company):
   > *Ike, JFK, Jos. Schlitz Brewing Co.*

   d. Number (in the serial sense only):
   > *No. 3 (*but *number one choice)*

  e. Political and state designation of legislators:
   Sen. Mary White (R-Pa.); Rep. John Black
   (Ind-Va.); Democratic Sens. Mary White (Pa.),
   John Black (N.Y.) and Peter Jones (Mich.)

  f. Ship and plane designations:
   USS Nautilus, SST

  g. The term *versus* when referring to lawsuits and
  court proceedings:
   Miranda v. Arizona (but *the Steelers versus the*
   Cardinals)

3. Do not abbreviate:

  a. Books of the Bible:
   Genesis 3:26

  b. Serial terms (except *No..* as in 2d above):
   Chapter 3, Figure 6, Page 21, Size 4A

  c. Vernacular used outside its normal section of the
  paper:
   RBIs (runs batted in, a sports term), *SDRs*
   (special drawing rights, a financial term)

4. Do not use such forms as *KO, OK, Xmas* and
Xway.

5. Do not use abbreviations in direct quotations except
for *Mr.* and *Mrs.* or unless the speaker actually spoke
the abbreviation.

  "Professor Black came to the U.S. in 1969 and,
  with Doctor Mary White, he founded the Acme
  Baking Company and became a leading citizen
  of Kansas City, Missouri," Jones said.

CAPITALIZATION

A. *Arts and letters*
B. *Doctrines, documents, legislation*
C. *Geography and natural features*
D. *Governmental organizations*
E. *Headlines*
F. *Manufactured features*
G. *Military services*
H. *Political parties*
I. *Political units*
J. *Proper names*
K. *Religion*
L. *Space*
M. *Titles*
N. *Trade names*
O. *Miscellany*

In general: Capitalization styles are largely arbitrary and vary greatly. But once decided on, the style should be consistent for all titles, all nations, all levels of activity; it should not be subject to exception or personal whim. The

Washington Post style is "up"; it leans toward full capitalization. Five basic rules apply: capitalize proper names in both full and short forms; capitalize titles preceding names; lowercase plurals, general references and derivatives; lowercase when in doubt; capitalize to avoid ambiguity or absurdity.

A. ARTS AND LETTERS

1. Capitalize principal words in titles of books, paintings, plays, sculpture, songs and television programs.

   Jessica Mitford's "The American Way of Death," Michelangelo's "David," "ABC Monday Night Football"

2. Capitalize musical compositions but lowercase references to key and instrumentation unless part of the title.

   Beethoven's Fifth Symphony (or Symphony No. 5), Schoenberg's Five Pieces for Orchestra, Mendelssohn's Concerto in E Minor for Violin, Mozart's Sinfonia Concertante in E flat major for violin and viola

3. Capitalize sections and movements of a musical composition only if part of the title; capitalize and abbreviate such references as opus and Koechel numbers (for Mozart compositions).

   Debussy's "Prelude to 'The Afternoon of a Faun,'" prelude to the third act of "Lohengrin"; Beethoven's "Egmont" Overture, overture to "The Marriage of Figaro"; Tchaikovsky's "Andante Cantabile," the andante movement; (Op. 16), (K. 124)

4. Capitalize artistic styles and movements but lowercase general references.

   Romanesque, Gothic, Federal, Beaux-Arts,

> *Bauhaus, Expressionist, Pointillist, Art
> Nouveau, Cubist, Dada, Op Art, Post-Romantic;*
> but *classical* (after Greek and Roman styles),
> *baroque* (extravagantly ornate), *rococo*
> (delicately ornamented), *gothic* (gloomy,
> forbidding), *modern* (spare, geometric)

5. Capitalize distinguishing words in titles and sections of publications, including the word *the* if it is part of the name.

> *The Washington Post, Style section, Metro staff,
> The Washington Post Co., The Post Co., The
> Times, Time magazine, The New York Times
> Magazine, Le Monde, Al Ahram, Der Spiegel*
> (but *sports section, editorial pages, financial
> writer*)

B. DOCUMENTS, DOCTRINES, LEGISLATION, ETC.

1. Capitalize historic documents, historic doctrines, important legal codes, enacted laws, ratified constitutional amendments and ratified treaties.

> *Magna Carta, Mayflower Compact, Constitution,
> Bill of Rights, U.N. Charter, Monroe Doctrine,
> Marshall Plan, Code Napoleon, Uniform Code
> of Military Justice, Taft-Hartley Act, 18th
> Amendment (Prohibition Amendment), Treaty of
> Versailles, SALT Treaty*

2. Lowercase pending or defeated legislation, general references and plurals.

> *welfare reform bill, nuclear accords, Bricker
> amendment, federal copyright law, First and
> Fifth amendments*

C. GEOGRAPHY AND NATURAL FEATURES

1. Capitalize geographic or descriptive regions.

> *Lower East Side* (of New York), *South Side* (of

Chicago), *West End* (of London), *Northeast* (quadrant of Washington, D.C.), *the Bowery, the Loop, East, East Coast, Atlantic Coast* (region, not shoreline), *Northern Virginia, Gulf Coast, Upstate New York, Eastern Shore* (of Maryland and Virginia), *Shenandoah Valley, Upper (and Lower) Peninsula of Michigan, Midwest, Middle West, Mountain States,* (Great) *Plains, Panhandle* (of Florida, Texas and Oklahoma), *Northern Hemisphere, Central Highlands, Mekong Delta, West Bank* (of the Jordan), *the Continent* (of Europe), *the Subcontinent* (of Asia), *Mideast, Far East, Southeast Asia, Occident, Orient, South Pacific, Temperate Zone, Arctic, Arctic Circle, Antarctic, Antarctica*

2. Capitalize specific natural features.

   Gulf Stream, Great Dismal Swamp, Potomac River, Lake Erie, Continental Divide, Grand Canyon, Rocky Mountains, San Andreas Fault, San Francisco Bay, Great Basin, Pacific Ocean

3. Capitalize fanciful terms for geographic and natural features.

   Down East (northeastern United States), *Bible Belt, Deep South, Corn Belt, Ho Chi Minh Trail, Down Under* (Australia)

4. Capitalize geographic features.

   17th Parallel, International Date Line, Equator, Mason-Dixon Line, North Pole

5. Lowercase mere direction, location and points of the compass.

   southern California, eastern seaboard, wind from the west, mid-Manhattan, inner city

6. Lowercase derivatives.

   easterner, plainsman, occidental, oriental (but

Oriental in the racial sense), *southern Californian, equatorial Africa*
7. Lowercase generic terms standing alone unless used in a familiar, poetic or stylized sense.
    the coast, the hemisphere, a boat on the bay; (but "For anyone born in the Islands . . . ")
8. Lowercase generic plurals.
    the Northern and Southern hemispheres, Chesapeake and Delaware bays
9. Lowercase mere descriptive terms.
    the volcano Popocatepetl, Maine shoreline, American continental shelf

D. GOVERNMENTAL ORGANIZATIONS

1. Capitalize proper or commonly accepted names for government organizations, including short forms.
    U.N. Security Council (Security Council), International Atomic Energy Commission, Presidium, House of Commons (Commons), Diet, Foreign Ministry, British Embassy, U.S. Mission, Senate, Cabinet, Ways and Means Committee, Department of State (State Department, State), Foreign Service, Office of Science and Technology, U.S. 4th Circuit Court of Appeals, General Assembly, City Council, Metropolitan Police Department, Department of Human Resources, Motor Vehicles Division, Board of Education, Board of Regents
2. Capitalize ad hoc, temporary and proposed bodies.
    Pay Board, Warren Commission, Electoral College, International Control Commission, Pilot Police District Project
3. Capitalize informal references.
    Ex-Im Bank, the Fed, the Hill

4. Lowercase divisions, sections, bureaus and similar components unless they are identifiable without reference to their parent bodies.

   antitrust division of the Justice Department, pest management section of the Maryland Agricultural Department (but *Navy Bureau of Medicine, Bureau of Labor Statistics, Chevrolet Division*)

5. Lowercase generic terms and partial references standing alone.

   the assembly, the board, the bureau, the committee, the council, the department, the embassy, the regents, the supervisors

6. Lowercase plurals.

   81st and 82nd congresses, departments of Justice and State, Alameda and Fresno counties

7. Lowercase informal terms.

   the administration, the appellate court, executive branch, government (except in formal diplomatic usage), *judicial branch, judiciary, legislative branch, legislature, lower house, ministry, parliament* (unless a proper name), *post office* (for U.S. Postal Service), *upper house, weather bureau* (for National Weather Service)

8. Lowercase informal names of legislative committees and names of subcommittees except for words referring to the parent committee.

   Senate rackets committee, Senate Judiciary subcommittee on refugees, House water resources subcommittee

9. Lowercase such words as *city*, *state* and *federal* except in reference to the legal entity or when used with an agency or title.

   the city boundaries, the state capital, the federal government; the City of Topeka sued . . . , the

City Board of Elections, State Sen. John Black, State Highway Administration, Federal Soil Conservation Service

10. Lowercase derivatives unless part of a proper name.
*congressional apathy (*but *Congressional Record), legislative branch, senatorial rhetoric, departmental business*

11. Lowercase parenthetical translations.
Bundestag (lower house of parliament)

12. Lowercase concepts as distinct from programs and agencies that administer them.
Americans have an advanced social security system and receive Social Security payments from the Social Security Administration. The Federal Reserve Board governs the Federal Reserve System. The American civil service is regulated by the Civil Service Commission, which conducts Civil Service tests.

E. HEADLINE CAPITALIZATION

1. Headline style varies from department to department at The Post, as it does at many papers. The Style section uses a free headline style. The Weekly sections capitalize only proper words. But most other sections follow traditional headline style.

2. In normal headline usage:

a. Capitalize the first word of every line and all other nouns, verbs, and modifiers and all prepositions of four or more letters:
President Sternly Warns
12 Defecting Senators
To Vote for Tax Bill

b. Capitalize both parts of a hyphenated compound if they are real words:
Able-Bodied, Sit-In, Cover-Up

    c. Lowercase a word following a hyphenated prefix unless it is a proper word (but always capitalize a word following the prefix *ex-*):
2 Micro-organisms Identified; Pro-Arab Policy; Ex-Aide, Ex-President

    d. Lowercase hyphenated suffixes:
Truman-like

    e. Lowercase articles *(a, an, the), to* in infinitives and two- and three-letter conjunctions and prepositions unless they begin a line or are used as a verb substitute or part of a verb phrase:
*President Wins a Key Test; Black to Retire Today; Black Defeated by White (*but *White Gets By Black)*

F. MANUFACTURED FEATURES

    1. Capitalize historic or well-known buildings, rooms, roads, bridges, parks and similar features.
Capitol, Rotunda (of the Capitol), *Dirksen Senate Office Building, White House (Executive Mansion), East Room, Oval Office, Metropolitan Police Headquarters, National Airport, Memorial Bridge, Jefferson Memorial, U.S. Courthouse, Austrian Chancery, Statehouse* (if so styled or known), *Three Rivers Stadium, Hoover Dam, Gov. Thomas E. Dewey Thruway, Wall Street, St. Lawrence Seaway, Oakland County Fairgrounds, Forest Lawn Cemetery, St. Louis Zoo, Mark Hopkins Hotel, Berlin Wall, Place de la Concorde, Hall of Mirrors, Red Square, Old City* (of Jerusalem)

    2. Lowercase generic terms standing alone in plurals or in descriptive use.
the hall, the fairground; 15th and K streets;

Yankee and Shea stadiums; an Ohio River bridge, the throne room

G. MILITARY SERVICES

1. Capitalize full and short forms of American and foreign services, but lowercase plurals and general references.

U.S. Army, a Navy jet, Marine Corps (the Marines), Air Force budget, Coast Guard, National Guard, Ready Reserve, Women's Army Corps, French Foreign Legion, Royal Air Force (but the British and French air forces, Washington's army, funds for a modern navy)

2. Capitalize specific bases, commands, schools and ships.

Carlisle Barracks, Andrews Air Force Base, Joint Chiefs of Staff, German General Staff, Seventh Fleet, U.S. Army in Europe (USAREUR), Army Materiel Command, Signal Corps, Americal Division, Charlie Company, Army War College, Air Force Academy, USS Constellation

3. Capitalize fanciful names for units.

Green Berets, Hell on Wheels, Bengal Lancers, Afrika Korps

4. Capitalize service and rank preceding a name.

Midshipman John Black, Air Force Lt. Mary White

5. Capitalize the informal names of servicewomen and put their services in all capitals.

Wac, Wave, Spar; WAC (Women's Army Corps), WAVES (Women Accepted for Volunteer Emergency Service), SPAR (Coast Guard Women's Reserve, based on the acronym for the motto "Semper Paratus [Always Ready]")

6. Capitalize major wars, battles and revolts.

Battle of Armegeddon, French Revolution, the War Between the States, Boxer Rebellion, Boer War, World War I (the Great War, First World War), Russian (or October or Bolshevik) Revolution, Battle of the Bulge, Tet Offensive, Six-Day War

7. Capitalize important positions and fronts.

Western Front (of World War I), Maginot Line, DEW (Distant Early Warning) Line

8. Lowercase references to individuals unless the term incorporates the name of the service.

soldier, sailor, airman, trooper, ranger, paratrooper, artilleryman, grenadier; marine, three marines (but "The Marines have landed," referring to the service); a Green Beret; a National Guardsman, the guardsman; an Army Reservist, the reservists, French Foreign Legionnaire, a legionnaire

H. POLITICS AND POLITICAL PARTIES

1. Capitalize political and quasi-political organizations or movements.

Democratic Party, New Left, National Liberation Front, Provisional Wing (of the Irish Republican Army)

2. Capitalize their conventions, principal bodies and officers.

Democratic National Convention, Republican Platform Committee, Communist Party Central Committee, Democratic National Chairman John Jones

3. Capitalize fanciful names.

Solid South, Grand Old Party, New Deal, New

Frontier, Tories, Old Guard, Young Turks, Red
(referring to communist)

4. Capitalize party members and adherents (as distinct
from the philosophy).
*Democrats, Republicans, Socialists,
Communists, Independents, Conservatives*

5. Lowercase political philosophies and forms of government.
*democratic principles, republican system,
conservative economics, independent bloc, the
left, right-wingers, black power, socialism,
communism, communist Hungary, communist
troops, a communist government*

I. POLITICAL UNITS

1. Capitalize specific towns, cities, counties, states,
provinces, nations and similar units.
*Waterford Township, Borough of Manhattan,
City of New York* (used in a formal or legal
context), *the District* (of Columbia), *Fairfax
City, Washington State, Quebec Province, Khmer
Republic, Republic of China, Swiss
Confederation, Duzbek Autonomous Region,
Dominion of Canada, Crown Colony of Hong
Kong, British Empire*

2. Capitalize alliances, blocs and similar groupings.
East and West (communist and capitalist
spheres), *North and South* (in Civil War and
Reconstruction days), *the Allies and Allied* (or
Axis) *powers* of World War II, *NATO nations,
Warsaw Pact powers, Group of 10* (industrial
nations), *the Commonwealth* (formerly the
British Commonwealth)

3. Capitalize administrative and political districts.
Ward 5, 18th Congressional District
4. Capitalize fanciful names.
Iron Curtain, Third World
5. Lowercase general references.
the city, the Tidewater district, the Virginia commonwealth (but *Commonwealth of Virginia* and the *Commonwealth* for the former British Commonwealth), *the nation, the empire, the free world*
6. Lowercase generic plurals.
the states of Mississippi and Alabama
7. Lowercase derivatives.
southern vote, western powers

J. PROPER NAMES
1. Capitalize commonly accepted proper names in both full and short forms, but lowercase *the* and general references. Proper names include those of:
a. Corporations and unions:
*the Ford Motor Co., Ford Motor; Penn Central; Columbia Broadcasting System (*but *the CBS network); United Auto Workers (*but *auto workers union); Teamsters Union, the Teamsters* (accepted for the International Brotherhood of Teamsters), *the union*
b. Civic, social and fraternal groups (but lowercase references to individual members unless to do so would cause an absurdity):
Knights of Columbus, the Knights, a knight; Springfield Boys Club, the Boys Club, the club; B'nai B'rith; Little League, little leaguer; Odd Fellows, an Odd Fellow; the Shrine, the Shriners, two shriners, a shriner; the Benevolent and Protective Order of Elks, an

*Elk, American Legion, American Legionnaire,
a legionnaire; Boy Scouts of America, the
Scouts, two boy scouts, a scout; Ku Klux Klan,
the Klan, a klansman*

c. Eras, epochs and historic events:
*Creation, Dark Ages, Renaissance, Victorian
Age, Early American, Industrial Revolution,
Prohibition, Jazz Age, Beer Hall Putsch, the
(Great) Depression, Cultural Revolution (but
biblical days, 20th century)*

d. Historic and traditional addresses:
*Gettysburg Address, "Cross of Gold" speech,
Kennedy's Inaugural Address, State of the
Union Message, State of the State Message,
the president's Economic Message*

e. Holidays and special days:
*New Year's Eve (and Day, but start of the new
year), Father's Day, Halloween, Washington's
Birthday, Yuletide, Mardi Gras, Election Day,
Inauguration Day, April Fool's Day*

f. Major sports events and organizations:
*World Series (the Series), Olympic Games (the
Games), Davis Cup, Rose Bowl, Super Bowl
(but Stanley Cup playoffs, Washington Star
international tennis championships,
homecoming game, bat night crowd)*

g. Schools, universities and their components:
*Jones Elementary School, Jones High School;
Harvard University, Harvard College,
Harvard Graduate School of Business
Administration (but Harvard business
school); Michigan State University at Oakland
(but Michigan State's Oakland campus)*

h. High honors and decorations but not professional
awards:

*Medal of Honor, Nobel Peace Prize, Nobel
Prize in chemistry, Pulitzer Prize for
international reporting* (but *employe
suggestion award, most valuable player,
all-pro, all-America)*

i. Races and ethnic groups:
Caucasian, Oriental, Negro, Hispanic (but
*white, black, caucasoid, negroid, yellow, red,
colored, brown)*

j. Fanciful and coined words and terms:
*Alexander the Great, the Union, the Colonies,
the Republic, the Windy City, the Buckeye
State, the Old Dominion, the Nation's Capital,
Stars and Stripes, Hurricane Hazel,
Leathernecks, Project Apollo, Zip Code, the
Street (Wall), Big Board, Big Steel, Fourth
Estate*

2. Lowercase generic terms used as plurals or in a
general or descriptive sense.
*the First and Fifth amendments, the most
famous inaugural address*

3. Lowercase proper names that have acquired independent meaning.
*paris green, oxford gray, portland cement,
manhattan* (cocktail)*, molotov cocktail* (gasoline
bomb)*, navy blue, chinese red, french cuff,
french fries, napoleon* (pastry)*, dutch door,
oriental rug, diesel engine, bunsen burner,
brussels sprouts, gatling gun, swiss cheese,
bermuda shorts, gestapo tactics* (but *the
Gestapo) a quisling*

K. RELIGION

1. Capitalize all recognized faiths and their adherents.
Christianity, Christendom, Christian; Judaism,

*Reform Jew, Orthodox Jew; Roman Catholic
Church* (but *the church*)*, a Catholic; Eastern
Rite and Eastern Orthodoxy* (branches of
Christianity)*; Methodist Church, a Methodist;
Mormon Church* (informal name for Church of
Jesus Christ of Latter-day Saints)*; Islam,
Muslims; Zen Buddhism; a Confucianist; Hindu*

2. Capitalize titles preceding a name, but lowercase
titles used alone.
    Pope Paul, Rabbi John Black (but *the pope, the
    archbishop of Canterbury, the cardinal, the
    rabbi*)

3. Capitalize proper nouns referring to divinity and
the devil.
    *God, Allah, Jehovah, Our Father, the Almighty,
    the Holy Spirit, Supreme Being, the Lord, the
    Savior, the Messiah* (referring to Jesus)*, Son of
    Man, Virgin Mary, Angel Gabriel, Satan,
    Lucifer, the Devil, Father of Lies*

4. Capitalize personal pronouns referring to the deity
(but not to the devil) and lowercase relative pronouns.
    Thee, Thy, Thou, He, His, Him (but *who, whose,
    whosoever*)

5. Lowercase general references to deities and devils.
    *a god, a messiah, a devil, a savior, a supreme
    being*

6. Capitalize holy days, holy books and doctrines but
lowercase rituals and services.
    *Christmas, Passover, Holy Week, High Holy
    Days, Ramadan; Creation, Immaculate
    Conception, Nativity, Sermon on the Mount,
    Resurrection; Apostle's Creed, Augsburg
    Confession; Bible, Talmud, Old Testament,
    Koran, Gospel* (but *gospel truth*)*, Scriptures* (but

mass, confession, communion, bar mitzvah, seder)

7. Capitalize religious orders and bodies.
Black Friars, Ursuline Sisters, College of Cardinals

8. Capitalize historic events.
Great Schism, Crusades, Protestant Reformation, First and Second Vatican councils (or Vatican I and II)

9. Capitalize specific places referred to in a religious context, but lowercase them in general reference.
Heaven, Paradise, the Great Beyond, Hades, Hell, Holy See, St. James Parish, Wailing Wall, Old City (of Jerusalem), *City of David, Promised Land (*but *he moved heaven and earth, war is hell)*

10. Lowercase religious derivatives and general usage.
biblical, talmudic, scriptural, holy, papal, pontiff, bible of baseball

L. SPACE

1. Capitalize planets, constellations and other heavenly features and bodies.
Venus, Milky Way, Sea of Tranquility, Van Allen Belt, Halley's Comet, Big Dipper

2. Capitalize earth in its context as a planet; lowercase it in general or figurative use.
a probe from Earth to Mars; the coldest place on earth; a spadeful of the good earth

3. Lowercase generic terms.
sun, moon, stars, planet, galaxy, heavens, outer space, solar system, ionosphere, universe

4. Lowercase derivatives.
venusian gases, martian atmosphere

M. TITLES

1. Capitalize titles denoting a hierarchical position or distinguishing role (as distinct from a mere job description) when they precede names.

President John Black, First Lady Mary White (of all states and nations), Ambassador at Large John Black, Senate Majority Leader John Black, Ways and Means Committee Chairwoman Mary White, Special Counsel John Black, Assistant Warden Mary White, County Executive John Black, School Superintendent Mary White, UMW Treasurer John Black, Acting Baseball Commissioner Mary White, Redskin Coach John Black, Chief Nurse Mary White, Supreme Allied Commander John Black, Platoon Leader Mary White, Imperial Potentate John Black, Klan Supreme Wizard John Black

2. Capitalize academic, military, professional, quasi-military, religious and royal titles of rank or authority preceding names.

Prof. John Black, Col. Mary White, Dr. John Black, Police Officer Mary White, Pope John, Queen Mary

3. Capitalize terms of address preceding names.

Mr. Black, Miss White, Herr Schwartz, Mlle. Blanche

4. Capitalize terms of salutation and protocol.

"Your Excellency, we refuse." In this newspaper's opinion, His Honor erred twice.

5. Capitalize sobriquets both preceding a name and alone.

Sultan of Swat Babe Ruth (the Sultan of Swat)

6. Capitalize short forms and plurals preceding names.

President Black, Prof. White, Gens. Black and White

7. Lowercase titles standing alone.
   the president, the first lady, the queen of England, the papal nuncio, the chairman (but *the Dalai Lama,* since he has no other name*)*
8. Lowercase plurals and general references.
   the two senators, no Democratic mayor
9. Lowercase hyphenated qualifying terms.
   President-elect Black, Attorney General-designate White
10. Lowercase titles used with ex- and former.
    former president John Black, ex-senator Mary White
11. Lowercase derivatives.
    presidential, senatorial, mayoral, papal
12. Lowercase job or role descriptions and temporary minor titles.
    administrative assistant John Black, White House telephone operator Mary White, Acme Co. spokesman John Black, Washington Post staff writer Mary White, Hollywood producer John Black, carnival chairman Mary White, campaign director John Black
13. Place long or unwieldy titles after the name and in lowercase.
    John Black, assistant to the vice president, spoke next.

N. TRADE NAMES

1. Capitalize trade names but use them only when essential to the story.
   The mayor purchased a $10,000 Lincoln Continental as his official car.
2. When a trade name is not essential, use a generic substitute. Typical trade names and substitutes include:

Alka-Seltzer—antacid tablet
Baggies—plastic bags
ChapStick—lip balm
Coca-Cola—cola drink
Dictaphone—dictation machine
Ex-Lax—laxative
Fiberglas—fiber glass
Formica—laminated plastic
Frigidaire—refrigerator
Jell-O—gelatin dessert
Kleenex—tissues
Levi's—jeans
Masonite—hardboard
Mixmaster—food mixer
Naugahyde—vinyl-coated fabric
Ping-Pong—table tennis
Plexiglas—acrylic plastic
Polaroid—camera or self-developing film
Prestone—antifreeze
Pyrex—heat-resistant glass
Q-Tips—cotton swabs
Saran Wrap—plastic wrap
Scotch Tape—cellophane tape or plastic tape
Styrofoam—plastic foam
Tabasco—pepper sauce
Technicolor—color movies
Vaseline—petroleum jelly
Xerox—duplicator, photo copier

O. MISCELLANY

1. Capitalize designating terms used before figures and letters.

   Vitamin B, Room 306, Figure 3, Rte: 123,
   Chapter 23, Model 4A, Page 20, Class A,
   Division II

2. Capitalize the first word of a quotation when it is a full sentence or thought, and precede it with a comma or colon.

   Franklin said, "A penny saved is a penny earned."

3. Capitalize initials and all letters of true acronyms but capitalize only the first letter of strained efforts to create a word or near-word.

   AFL-CIO, ITT, UNESCO, SCORE, NOW (but *Geico, Citgo, Amvets, Amtrak, Conrail*)

4. Capitalize breeds of animals but lowercase the noun.

   Persian lamb, Airedale terrier, Shetland pony, Percheron horse, German shepherd, Hereford cattle (but *Great Dane*)

5. Capitalize distinguishing names of flowers; in Latin, capitalize the genus.

   Peace rose; camellia, Thea japonica

6. Capitalize personifications for stylistic effect.

   For Nature wields her scepter mercilessly

7. Lowercase government, trade and professional terms not commonly accepted as proper nouns, even if known by initials.

   consumer price index, gross national product (GNP), home edition, petrodollar

8. Lowercase the seasons and references to time.

   winter, autumn, daylight saving time, a.m., p.m.

9. Capitalize all parts of anglicized foreign surnames unless another preference is known; in foreign usage the article is usually lowercase unless the surname is used alone.

   Fiorello La Guardia, Charles de Gaulle, De Gaulle

NUMERALS

A. *Ordinary usage*
B. *When to use figures*
C. *When to spell out*
D. *Roman numerals*
E. *Large numbers*
F. *Punctuation of numerals*
G. *Miscellany*
H. *Metric units and conversions*

In general: It is easier to understand numbers expressed in figures than in words. As a rule, spell out numbers one through nine in ordinary text. Use figures for higher numbers and for statistical and sequential forms. Arabic numerals are easier to read than roman numerals; use the latter sparingly.

A. ORDINARY USAGE

1. Spell out numbers one through nine and use figures for numbers 10 and higher.

one horse, 10 customers

2. Apply the rule to both cardinal forms (one, two . . .)
and ordinal forms (first, second . . .).
   First Amendment, 15th Amendment
3. Use arabic numerals (1, 2, 3, 4, 5, 6, 7, 8, 9, 0) unless
roman numerals are specified (see D3).

B. WHEN TO USE FIGURES
1. In addresses (but use the nine-and-under rule for
streets).
   7 Stevens Ave. (but 7 Ninth St., 7 51st St.)
2. In ages.
   *2 months old, at age 3, aged 9 (but his third
   birthday)*
3. In dates, years, decades and centuries.
   *Jan. 3, 3rd of January; 1947, '47; the 1940s, the
   '40s (but Gay Nineties, Roaring Twenties); 5th
   century (but America's third century)*
4. In decimals, fractions and percentages larger than
one or in a series.
   *6.5 magnitude, 3½ laps, 5 percent interest,
   readings of 6.21, .02 and 0.14 (but three-tenths,
   three-quarters full, one-half percent)*
   NOTES: Convert awkward fractions to decimals when
   feasible. Use the form *12 one-hundredths*, not *twelve
   one-hundredths*. Use the form *5 percent*, not *5% or 5
   pct.*, except in headlines and tables.
5. In decisions, rulings, scores and votes.
   *a 5-to-4 decision, ruled 5 to 4, defeated the
   White Sox, 5-4, defeated the amendment by a
   vote of 6 to 4 (but by a two-vote margin)*
   NOTE: All such uses except sports scores require the
   word *to*.
6. In dimensions and measurements containing two or
more elements.
   5 feet 10 inches tall, 5-10 man, a 9-by-12 foot

rug, 2 feet by 1 foot 8 inches (but four feet tall, a
seven-footer, a snowfall of five inches, three ems)

7. In geographic and political districts.

   Zone 3, 2nd Precinct, 8th Congressional District,
   4th U.S. Circuit Court of Appeals

8. In mathematical usage.

   multiply by 4, divide by 6

9. In military and quasi-military ranks and terms.

   Airman 1st Class John Black, 2nd Lt. Mary
   White (but White is a second lieutenant),
   6-pounder, 33 mm, .38-caliber bullet, M16 rifle,
   5th Corps, 6th Fleet

10. In monetary units.

    5 cents (not 5¢ or $.05), $2 bill, 8 pounds, 6
    pesos, $1 million

11. In odds, proportions and ratios.

    a 15-1 longshot, 3 parts cement to 1 part water,
    1-3-5, 2 tablespoons of sugar to 1 cup of milk
    (but one chance in three)

12. In designations of planes, ships, spacecraft and vehicles.

    B1, Queen Elizabeth 2, Apollo 8, Viking 2,
    Formula 2 racer

    NOTE: Use arabic numerals unless roman numerals are part of a trade name (as in *Continental Mark IV*).

13. In sequential designations of acts, channels, chapters, courses, figures, models, rooms, routes, pages, positions, scales, sizes, speeds, etc.

    Act 1, Channel 5, Chapter 4, Philosophy 6,
    Figure 2, Model 1A, Room 8, Rte. 5, Page 9, No.
    2 position, 5 on the Richter scale, Size 3, 4 miles
    an hour, 7 to 9 knots

14. In sports scores, standings and standards (but follow the nine-and-under rule otherwise).

83-78, down 2, up 3, led 3-2, 4-5-1 record, par 3, 5-handicap, a jump of 25-10½, a time of 3:36.2 (but four-yard line, third and two, six-yard run, went three for four, connected on eight of 12 passes, seventh hole, two-pointer)

NOTE: In sports agate listings, figures may be used at will.

15. In technical terminology.

3.5 lens opening, 9 degrees latitude, Mach 2

16. In temperatures.

6 degrees (but *zero* and *6 below zero* rather than *–6* except in a series or table)

17. In time references.

4 p.m., 5 o'clock, 5 in the afternoon, 8 hours 30 minutes and 20 seconds (no commas), *a winning time of 3:36.2, a 4:10 mile*

C. WHEN TO SPELL OUT

1. In the case of single and related numbers at the start of a sentence.

Forty-three coal miners died. Forty to fifty coal miners died.

NOTE: Sentences can often be recast to avoid starting with a number.

2. In indefinite usage.

a hundred percent wrong, a thousand and one ways, temperatures in the thirties, in his seventies, twentyfold, sixty-odd

3. In formal language.

threescore years and ten, in the year nineteen hundred and seventy-seven

4. In figures of speech.

number one choice, Air Force One, Ten Commandments, Twelve Apostles, Gay Nineties, wouldn't touch it with a ten-foot pole

5. In fractions below one which stand alone.

*one-half inch, half an inch, one-half (*but
¹/₂-inch pipe, 3¹/₂ times, 35 one-thousandths)

6. In the case of figures separated by only a space or comma.

*ten 15-room houses (*instead of *10 15-room houses)*

D. ROMAN NUMERALS

1. The roman numerals are *I* (1), *V* (5), *X* (10), *L* (50), *C* (100), *D* (500), and *M* (1,000).

2. A repeated letter repeats its value; a letter following one of greater value adds to it; a letter preceding one of greater value subtracts from it; a dash over a letter increases its value a thousandfold. For example, XXIX equals 29, LXXXIX equals 89, MD equals 1,500 and V̄ equals 5,000.

3. Use roman numerals for lineal designations of persons and animals and in proper names if so specified. Use arabic numerals for all other lineal designations and for subdivisions of larger units.

John Black III (unless he prefers *3* or *3rd*), *King George III, Pope Pius XII, Native Dancer II, "The Godfather, Part II," Continental Mark IV, Phantom II, Chapter 20 of II Samuel;* but *Super Bowl 12, Formula 2 racer, Apollo 11, 5th Corps, Hamlet 3:2*

E. LARGE NUMBERS

1. Round off or approximate large numbers if it will help the reader and if the precise figure is not essential, particularly in headlines.

the president's $2,765,493,800 aid request (first reference); *the $2.8 billion request* (subsequent or casual references and in headlines)

2. In referring to millions, billions and so on, use a figure-word combination.

4 million people, $5.5 billion, $50 billion to $60

billion (or $50-60 billion but not $50 to $60 billion)

F. PUNCTUATION OF NUMERALS

1. In modifiers containing figures, hyphenate the compound.

   eight-hour day (not 8-hour), 10-foot board, 5-foot-6 girl (but a girl 5 feet 6)

2. Use apostrophes for omissions but not in plurals.

   class of '47, in the '50s (but B52s)

3. In spelling out numbers, use no commas and hyphenate only after words ending in *y.*

   one hundred seventy-five

4. In four-digit and larger numbers, place a comma to the left of each group of three digits, but do not use commas in addresses, phone numbers, serial numbers and so on.

   1,347,685 citizens (but 1347 Oak St. and #1347685)

G. MISCELLANY

1. Use figures in a series of three or more numbers any one of which is larger than 10.

   6 goats, 8 sheep and 12 horses (but eight sheep and 12 horses, Second and 15th amendments)

2. Rephrase to avoid confusing juxtaposition of figures.

   12 of the 32 approved (not of the 32, 12 approved)

3. In proper names, use the preferred form if known.

   Twentieth Century Fund, 20th Century-Fox

4. Spell out numbers in fanciful usage.

   Arizona State eleven, Big Ten, Chicago Seven, Pacific Eight

5. Do not use *about, approximately* or *-odd* with precise figures. Never use *some* with figures.

6. In headlines: Generally use figures but spell out *one* (except for scores and votes); use the form *3-2* for votes, not *3 to 2*; use the form *5%* or *5 Pct.*, not *5 percent*; use the short form for ordinals (*2d, 3d*) if necessary to make headline a fit.

H. METRIC STYLE GUIDE AND CONVERSION TABLE

1. Common prefixes for metric units.

mega (M): a factor of one million
kilo (k): a factor of one thousand
centi (c): a factor of one one-hundredth
milli (m): a factor of one one-thousandth
micro (μ): a factor of one one-millionth

2. Metric units and approximate equivalents.

a. Area.

Hectare (ha)—2.5 acres

b. Length.

kilometer (km)—0.6 mile
meter (m)—39.5 inches
centimeter (cm)—about 0.4 inch
millimeter (mm)—about 1/40 inch

c. Pressure.

kilopascal (kPa)—atmospheric pressure is about 1000 kPa

d. Temperature (expressed in Celsius degrees, named after the Swedish astronomer who invented the centigrade system).

water's freezing point—0°C (32°F)
water's boiling point—100°C (212°F)
normal body temperature—37°C (98.6°F)
normal room temperatures—20-25°C (68-77°F)

e. Volume.

liter (L)—one quart and two ounces
milliliter (mL)—one-fifth teaspoon

    f. Weight.
        metric ton (t)—long ton (2,240 pounds)
        kilogram (kg)—2.2 pounds
        gram (g)—about $1/28$ ounce

3. Conversion factors.
    a. Area.
        from square miles to square kilometers: × 2.6
        from acres to hectares: × 0.4
        from square yards to square meters: × 0.8
        from square feet to square meters: × 0.09
        from square inches to square centimeters:
        × 6.5
    b. Length.
        from miles to kilometers: × 1.6
        from yards to meters: × 0.9
        from feet to centimeters: × 30
        from inches to centimeters: × 2.54
    c. Pressure.
        from inches of mercury to kilopascals: × 3.4
        from pounds per square inch to kilopascals:
        × 6.9
    d. Temperature.
        from Fahrenheit to Celsius: × $5/9$ after
        subtracting 32
    e. Volume.
        from cubic yards to cubic meters: × 0.76
        from cubic feet to cubic meters: × 0.03
        from gallons to liters: × 3.8
        from quarts to liters: × 0.95
        from pints to liters: × 0.47
        from cups to liters: × 0.24
        from fluid ounces to milliliters: × 30
        from cubic inches to milliliters: × 16
        from tablespoons to milliliters: × 15
        from teaspoons to milliliters: × 5

f. Weight.

 from short tons (2,000 lbs.) to metric tons: ×
 0.9

 from pounds to kilograms: × 0.45

 from ounces to grams: × 28

122

PUNCTUATION

In general: The primary purpose of punctuation is to clarify written expression. Tend toward open punctuation (fewer marks) if the meaning is clear. Use common sense and avoid following rules blindly.

A. AMPERSAND (&)

The ampersand takes the place of *and* but is used only in prescribed forms.

1. Use an ampersand in abbreviations of organizations.
   AT&T, C&O Canal, Texas A&I
2. Use an ampersand in tables and similar listings if necessary to save space.
3. Use an ampersand if it is part of a proper name.
   Procter & Gamble, Ringling Bros. and Barnum & Bailey Circus, U.S. News & World Report (but American Telephone and Telegraph Co.)

B. APOSTROPHE (')

The apostrophe is used to form contractions, plurals and possessives and to indicate omissions.

1. Contractions.
   a. Use an apostrophe in common contractions.
      I've, you've, he's, can't, it's, wouldn't, you're
   b. Use an apostrophe in capital-letter verbs (although such forms should seldom if ever be used).
      Champ KO'd, MC'ing the show, Senate OK's
   c. Do not use an apostrophe in the possessives *hers, its, theirs* and *yours.*
   d. Do not use an apostrophe in contractions of words in common use.
      chute, copter, gator, phone, possum, round
2. Plurals.
   a. Use an apostrophe in forming plurals of single lowercase letters.
      Mind your p's and q's.
   b. Do not use an apostrophe in forming other plu-

rals of letters, numbers, words standing for numbers or non-nouns.

the ABCs, two PhDs, the three Rs, three As and two Bs, a column of 2s, back in the 1920s, three B52s, shot in the low 80s, count by fours, no ifs, ands or buts (but do's and don'ts)

3. Possessives.

a. Use *'s* after nouns not ending in *s*, but use only *'* after nouns ending in *s*.

girl's, girls'; GI's, GIs'; woman's, women's; princess', princesses'; Jones', Joneses'; Congress', Jesus'

NOTE: Words ending in *z* take *'s* (*Lopez's band, jazz's beginnings*).

b. Use *'s* for the possessive of titles and initials and figures.

King George V's reign, Ford Motor Co.'s Tokyo office, B52's cockpit

c. Use an apostrophe with indefinite pronouns but not with possessive pronouns.

someone's, each other's (but his, hers)

d. Use a single apostrophe to show common possession but use separate apostrophes to show separate possession.

John and Mary's house, John's and Mary's clothes

e. Use an apostrophe in established idiomatic phrases that take the possessive even though there is no actual ownership.

a day's wages, John's service, two hours' travel time, a stone's throw, for pity's sake, in case of the train's leaving, for old times' sake, week's end

f. Omit the apostrophe in proper nouns unless the possessive aspect is clear, but follow established usages.

Actors Equity, State Teachers College, Harpers Ferry (but *White's Ferry, Pike's Peak, New Year's Day, Court of St. James's, Prince George's County, Mother's Day*)

g. Omit the apostrophe where usage is more descriptive than possessive.

printers union

h. Follow ordinary style in possessive phrases.

a friend of hers, a friend of Julia's

4. Omissions.

a. Use an apostrophe to indicate omissions in quoted colloquial speech and phrases and in poetic usage.

"An' one of 'em is the new boss." "His name is Dan'l." Y'all, rock 'n' roll, wash 'n' wear, o'er the rainbow

b. Use an apostrophe to indicate omitted numbers.

in the '30s, class of '47, Spirit of '76

c. Use an apostrophe (sparingly) in headlines to indicate omitted letters.

M'Namara, M'Donald (but never before a lowercase letter as in *Macmillan*)

C. BRACKETS (see PARENTHESES)

D. COLON (:)

The colon is used to introduce something that follows (such as an amplification, an example, a list, a question or a quotation).

1. Use a colon to introduce lists, tabulations, texts, etc.

Among the invited were: . . . . He made four points: . . . . The text of the communique: . . . .

2. Use a colon preceding direct quotation of one or more sentences.

The president put it this way: "We shall win."

3. Use a colon in script-type dialogue.
   Jones: Did you? Smith: I refuse to answer.
4. Use a colon for effect or emphasis.
   Said Jesus: "I shall go." Today is the dead center of the year: 182 days gone, 182 days to go.
5. Use a colon to mark discontinuity.
   The question came up: What would he do now?
6. Use a colon in place of *for instance.*
   Several outcomes were possible: injury, exposure to danger, even death.
7. Use a colon before a final clause summarizing preceding matter.
   To be born, to live, to die: that is our fate.
8. Use a colon after a salutation.
   Mr. Chairman:, My dear sir:
9. Use a colon to indicate biblical chapter and verse.
   Matthew 2:6
10. Use a colon to separate hours and minutes in clock time and elapsed time (but use a period to separate minutes and seconds).
    10:30 p.m., a winning time of 2:31.33
11. Lowercase the first word after a colon except when it is a proper name or when it begins a complete and independent sentence (not just a complementary one).
    The answer came quickly: We shall never go.
    There was no lack of courage: his chances were zero.

E. COMMA (,)

It is impossible to lay down a complete set of rules for use of the comma. As a general rule, omit commas where possible. But common sense should dictate usage, and clarity should be the goal.

1. Use commas in a series but not before the conjunction.

    red, white, green and blue; 1, 2 or 3

2. Use commas to set off attribution of a statement.

    The path, he said, is difficult.

3. Use commas to set off words in apposition.

    Secretariat, the favorite, was scratched.

4. Use a comma between independent clauses to clarify or to avoid confusion.

    The general said goodbye to the troops, and the parade was history.

5. Use commas to set off terms of address.

    Mr. Chairman, I protest. Yes, sir, I do.

6. Use a comma to separate words or figures that might otherwise be misunderstood.

    The question is, is it workable? Instead of 50, 20 came.

7. Use a comma to indicate omission of a word or words.

    Then we had much; now, nothing.

8. Use commas to set off figures in apposition.

    The House approved the bill, 202 to 201, in a cliffhanger. The bill won, 202 to 201, in a cliffhanger. The House vote, 202 to 201, was a cliffhanger (but The House voted 202 to 201 in a cliffhanger). The Yankees beat the Indians, 5–2.

9. Use commas in numbers over 999 but not in addresses, serial numbers, phone numbers, etc.

    1,234 horses (but 1234 Oak St. and No. 12345678)

10. Use commas after the day and year in precise dates (but omit commas when only the month and day or month and year are used.)

    The letter of Jan. 19, 1977, was lost. (But the Jan. 19 letter and the January 1977 letter.)

11. Use commas to set off ages, geographical designations, titles.

> *Black, 29, who was named dean; the*
> *Louisville, Ky., group; White, the bureau chief,*
> *reported . . .*

12. Omit commas before indirect quotations.

> *The mayor said (,) that the issue was moot.*

13. Omit commas before roman numerals, *Sr., Jr., Inc.,
Ltd.*, degrees and religious order designations.

> *Queen Elizabeth II, John Black Jr., Acme*
> *Products Inc., John Black SJ*

14. Omit commas in multiunit measures of height, weight, time, latitude and the like.

> *stood 5 feet 6 inches, weighed 3 pounds 6*
> *ounces, flew there in 2 hours 19 minutes, a ship*
> *located at 40 degrees 19 minutes 4 seconds west*

15. Omit commas before *of* phrases except in cases of apposition.

> *Queen Elizabeth of England, chairman John*
> *Black of Acme Inc. (*but *Mary White, of*
> *Philadelphia, and John Black, of 1234 Oak*
> *St.)*

16. Omit commas between two nouns when one identifies the other.

> *the painter Van Gogh, the opera "Aïda," his*
> *wife Sally and daughter Linda*

NOTE: Technically, the absence of commas around *Sally* suggests he is a bigamist, but common sense tells us otherwise. Similarly, Linda may or may not be his only daughter; we often do not know.

17. Omit commas around restrictive clauses and phrases (which are essential to the sense of the sentence and cannot be dropped) but use commas around nonrestrictive clauses and phrases (which add details but can be dropped).

*Prisoners who have served a year will be
released tomorrow. The prisoners, who heard the
news with cheers, prepared to leave their cells.*

NOTE: A frequent error is omission of the comma at
the end of a nonrestrictive clause.

18. Omit commas around short transitional or introductory expressions. But use commas for emphasis or if one would normally tend to pause in speaking at that point.

    *She had indeed left. Obviously she had no
    intention of going. He had naturally refused.
    (But: Meanwhile, the president left.)*

19. Put commas inside quotation marks (both single and double).

    *"I cannot," he said. "She said, 'I won't,'" he
    repeated.*

20. Reconstruct sentences to avoid using too many commas.

POOR	BETTER
The woman, incurably ill, police said, shot herself.	*Police said the incurably ill woman shot herself.*

F. DASH (—)

Dashes are used to indicate abrupt changes in thought, continuity and pace. A pair of dashes can often be used in place of commas or parentheses and a single dash in place of a colon, but they should be used sparingly. An ordinary em dash is typewritten as two hyphens with a space before and after (--); it is set in type as a solid dash without spaces.

1. Use dashes to indicate a sharp turn in thought, a significant pause, uncertainty and interpolation.

    *I've been waiting for—ah, I see her now. After
    three years we found him—in jail! I—hope so. If*

the ship sinks—God forbid—he will be a ruined man.

2. Use dashes to indicate apposition, particularly if use of commas would be confusing.

   Bewildered by the Spanish landing—their first sight of foreigners—the natives began throwing spears.

3. Use dashes in enumeration and preceding a summary phrase.

   The three of them—John, Mary and Paul—went to Europe. Mountains, prairies and cities—these are America.

4. Use dashes with divided quotations (but be careful where they go).

   "My son"—his tone was grave—"is missing."

   "My son—" he stammered, "my son is missing."

5. Use a dash in listing years of birth and death.

   (1896—1917), (1916—   )

6. Use a dash in logotypes.

   NEW YORK (AP)—The first snowfall was heavy.

7. Use a dash between quotation and the author's name.

   ". . . for your country."—John F. Kennedy

8. Use a closed-up dash as a minus sign in temperatures (but the form *18 below* or *18 below zero* is better).

   It fell to –18 in Duluth.

9. Use a two-em dash to indicate an incomplete quotation or omitted letters in a word. (Signify a two-em dash by typing four hyphens and writing "2-em dash" above them in a circle.)

   "My God, it's ——!" the mystery witness was Miss R——.

G. ELLIPSIS (. . .)

The ellipsis (properly called points of ellipsis or ellipsis periods) is used to indicate omission of words or sentences. It is used most often to remove unimportant or irrelevant matter from quotations or texts. An ellipsis is typewritten as three spaced periods (. . .) but printed without spaces.

1. Use ellipsis to indicate omission in quotations or text.

   "The first thing . . . is to hire him," Black said.

2. Use an ellipsis in stylized writing to string together unrelated items.

   John Black is the favorite to start the game at fullback . . . The next World Series should be the richest yet . . .

3. Do not use an ellipsis in place of commas or dashes to indicate a pause, emphasis or apposition.

4. Do not use an ellipsis to indicate an omitted profanity or obscenity: use hyphens (see IV H).

5. When an ellipsis is used at the start of a quotation, capitalize the first word.

   " . . . The first priority for the nation. . . . "

6. When an ellipsis is used at the end of a sentence, add a fourth point as a period or use other terminal punctuation.

   "It shall be done. . . . " "We have no choice. . . !"
   "But where can we go. . . ?"

H. EXCLAMATION POINT (!)

Exclamation points are rarely used in news stories except in quotations and stylized or personalized copy.

1. Use exclamation points to indicate surprise, appeal, incredulity or other strong emotion and to signify irony.

> *How wonderful! John, please hurry! I can't*
> *believe it! You don't mean it!*

2. Do not use other terminal punctuation after an exclamation point.

   > *"Let's go!" he shouted.*

3. If an exclamation occurs at the end of a question, use the more appropriate punctuation in each case.

   > *"Did you hear them shouting 'Resign! Resign!*
   > *Resign!'" "Do you know the song 'Hello, Dolly'?"*

I. HYPHEN (-) AND COMPOUND WORDS

Questions of when and how to use compounds—formed either by hyphenating words or running them together—drive even experts to despair. The U.S. Government Printing Office stylebook devotes two chapters and no fewer than 58 pages to compounds. The Oxford University Press stylebook remarks, "If you take hyphens seriously, you will surely go mad." Dictionaries disagree about compounding. So too do veteran copy editors (indeed, should it be *copy editors*, *copy-editors* or *copyeditors*?). Word formation changes according to sense (*hairbrush* but obviously not *camel's-hairbrush*) and part of speech (*air conditioner* but *to air-condition*). But even if rules are impossible to devise, hyphenation and compounding must be taken seriously as an aid to comprehension. *Webster's New World* is the Washington Post authority for compounding, but these guidelines may be useful.

1. Do not compound words if they appear in regular order, if their meaning is clear and if compounding would not improve comprehension.

   > *atomic energy bill, half dozen, double play ball,*
   > *social security legislation.*

2. Do compound words for ease of reading, to avoid

ambiguity, to clarify figurative or improvised usage, and to express a single thought that the words do not express when used separately.

pay-as-you-go plan, happy-go-lucky, firm-mattress manufacturer, small-business profits, high-speed line, large-scale project, forget-me-not, half-baked, one-person-one-vote principle, afterglow, whitewash

3. Compound nouns are usually run together in noun-noun form and hyphenated in adjective-noun and verb-noun forms. Nouns usually are not compounded in noun-adjective form.

bookbinder, fundraiser, blue-pencil, cure-all, heir apparent (but *knight-errant*)

4. Compound verbs are usually hyphenated.

to cold-shoulder, to soft-pedal

5. Modifiers may be hyphenated, run together or not compounded, depending on their use.

a. Generally hyphenate a compound modifier preceding the word modified.

far-reaching program, drought-stricken area, five-under-par 67, 20-cent cigar, well-known teacher, U.S.-owned warehouse

b. Generally do not hyphenate a compound modifier used in the predicate if its last element is a participle.

The program was far reaching. The area was drought stricken.

c. Generally do not hyphenate a compound modifier whose first element is a comparative or superlative.

lower income neighborhood, best liked books (but *lowercase type, bestselling book*)

d. Generally do not hyphenate a compound modifier whose first element is an adverb ending in *ly*.

*eagerly awaited speech, totally inept
performance*

e. Generally do not hyphenate proper nouns used as
modifiers unless the first one ends in *o* or unless
they designate a joint relationship.

*Italian American neighborhood, Italo-
American neighborhood, Italian-
American treaty; two Hispanic Americans,
Latin America trip, French Canadian separatists,
South Carolina roads; Afro-American, Anglo-
Saxon, Franco-Prussian; Richmond-
Washington road, French-Irish-English descent.*

f. Do not hyphenate foreign phrases used as modifiers.

ante bellum days, per diem allowance

g. Retain hyphens in suspended compounds (in
which the basic element is omitted in all but the
last term).

5-, 10- and 20-foot sections

NOTE: It often is preferable to avoid suspended
compounds altogether by recasting the sentence.

6. Prefixes are increasingly run together with root
words.

a. Generally do not use a hyphen with: *a, ante, anti,
bi, by, circum, co, counter, dis, down, electro,
extra, fore, hydro, hyper, hypo, in, infra, inter,
intra, mal, micro, mid, multi, non, off, on, out,
over, pan, post, pre, re, semi, sesqui, sub, super,
supra, trans, tri, ultra, un, under, uni, up.
amoral, anteroom, antimissile, biweekly, bylaw,
circumnavigate, coauthor, counteraction,
disassociate, downstream, electromagnet,
extramarital, foregoing, hydroelectric,
hypercritical, hypodermic, inaccessible, infrared,
intermingle, intramural, maladjusted,*

*microbiology, midday, multimillionaire,
noncommittal, offset, oncoming, outargue,
overrate, pansophism, postwar, prearrange,
retell, semitropical, sesquicentennial, subhuman,
superhighway, supraorbital, transoceanic,
triennial, ultraviolet, unbreakable,
underdeveloped, unicycle, upend*

b. Generally use a hyphen with: *all, no, quasi, self* and *wide.*

*all-round, no-trump, quasi-judicial,
self-government, wide-open*

c. Use a hyphen with *ex* only when it means "former" and join it with a noun, not a modifier.

*ex-secretary (*but *excommunicate), ex-secretary
of HUD (*not *ex-HUD secretary)*

d. Use a hyphen to avoid doubling vowels except after short prefixes *(co, de, pre, pro, re).*

*anti-inflation, micro-organisms,
semi-independent (*but *cooperate, deemphasize,
reelect)*

e. Use a hyphen to avoid ambiguity.

co-op (joint venture), *re-cover* (cover again)

f. Use a hyphen to separate duplicated prefixes.

re-redirect

g. Use a hyphen to join prefixes to capitalized words unless the combined form has acquired independent meaning.

*anti-British, un-American, pre-Columbia (*but *transatlantic, antisemitic)*

7. Suffixes are generally run together with the root word, but a hyphen is used with proper names, to avoid tripling a consonant and to clarify sense.

lifelike, Truman-like, bell-like, lean-to, mop-up

8. Compounds ending in such generic terms as *boat, fish, house, keeper, man, mate, owner, proof, room,* *shop, tight, wise, work* and *yard* (and many others) are generally run together.

oreboat, codfish, bathhouse, beekeeper, doorman, helpmate, homeowner, foolproof, laundryroom, workshop, bookstore, watertight, streetwise, busywork, brickyard

9. Do not use a hyphen in titles except to indicate combined offices or nonincumbency.

vice president, secretary of state, attorney general, delegate at large, ambassador at large, commander in chief, assistant professor, editor in chief (but *secretary-treasurer, president-elect, secretary-designate, ex-governor*)

10. Generally use hyphens in these other instances:

a. To indicate joint relationships:
blue-green feathers, city-county cooperation, Taft-Hartley Act

b. To join conflicting or repetitive elements:
comedy-ballet, pitter-patter, walkie-talkie

c. With figurative compound expressions using an apostrophe in the first element:
bull's-eye, cat's-paw, crow's-nest, camel's-hair

d. To join a single capital letter to a noun or participle:
H-bomb, T-shaped, U-boat, V-necked, X-raying

e. To join prepositional-phrase compounds of three or more words:
government-in-exile, jack-in-the-box, mother-in-law, mother-of-pearl (but *coat of arms, next of kin*)

f. To join compound numbers and fractions:
twenty-five, 6-4 forward, 4-1 odds, 20-20 vision, three-quarters (but *three one-hundredths, 4½, a share of one half*)

g. To join modifiers in number-word form (but not

in word-number or letter-number form except for federal road numbers):
60-watt bulb, ¹/₂-inch drill (but *uranium 235, Formula 2 racer, B52, Mark IV, Rte. 606, US-40, I-75*)
NOTE: Preferred style is *4-H Club* and *7-Eleven store*.)

J. PARENTHESES (( )) AND BRACKETS ([ ])

1. In general, parentheses are used by a writer to indicate interpolation in his or her own copy; brackets are used by an editor to interpolate material from another source. But editors should use parentheses to interpolate routine material that a writer merely forgot to include.
2. In particular use parentheses to enclose:
   a. Incidental comment:
      They were nearly home (after five days of driving) and their spirits rose.
   b. Nicknames:
      Julius (Doctor J) Erving
   c. Fuller identification:
      "I told (Prime Minister John) Black that he was wrong."
   d. A political-geographic designation:
      Sen. Mary White (D-Conn.)
   e. Figures or letters in a series:
      The water is: (a) clear, (b) muddy, (c) polluted. He said he is resigning because of (1) age, (2) health and (3) boredom.
   f. A specific location in ambiguous designations:
      the Springfield (Ohio) City Council
   g. Equivalents and translations:
      It cost 300 lire ($5.60). The Diet (parliament) approved it. Germany's famed autobahn

(expressway) system is well maintained.
h. Explanatory material:
Q: What (handing the witness a list) is this?
i. The source in a dateline:
NEW YORK (AP)—

3. In particular use brackets to enclose:
   a. Reference keys within the story:
   [Treasury Secretary John Black called the plan unworkable. Page A23]
   b. Material from another writer, service or dateline:
   [Washington Post staff writer Mary White reported from Chicago that . . .] [Associated Press put the total at 125 and said it might reach 250.] [In Washington, the State Department said . . .]
   c. Later developments in a datelined story where there might be some confusion about time or sequence:
   [But three hours later the plane was still on the ground, AP reported.]
   d. An interpolation that did not come from the speaker or writer:
   " . . . but when I saw Black [John Black, president of the firm], I learned . . . "

   NOTE: Except for incidental matter within a sentence, bracketed material should be paragraphed.

4. Do not overdo the use of parentheses and brackets.
   a. They are not needed with simple background information.
   b. Brackets can often be eliminated by using the credit "From News Services" instead of a single credit, by removing the dateline and crediting sources internally or by using a shirttail to credit additional sources.

    c. Limit the number of interpolated paragraphs (one or two long ones are better than a half dozen short ones) and run them consecutively, if possible, rather than scattering them.

5. When two or more paragraphs are interpolated, all take an opening parenthesis or bracket but only the last one takes a closing parenthesis or bracket.

6. In quoted matter use dashes, not parentheses, to set off incidental comments and asides.

    "I feel strongly—but I'll never know, will I?—that I could have won in 1976," he said.

K. PERIOD (.)

1. Use periods after declarative sentences and rhetorical questions.

    He went. Why don't we go.

2. Use periods in decimals and percentages and between dollars and cents.

    3.23, .345 percent, $12.15

3. Use periods in most lowercase and capital-lowercase abbreviations (see Chapter VI).

    p.m., v., c.o.d., Mr., Jr., (but *mph*)

4. Omit periods in most uppercase abbreviations (see Chapter VI).

    UAR, FBI, GI, MP, UNESCO, CORE, COPE, AFL-CIO (but *U.S., D.C., U.N.*)

5. Do not use periods in question-and-answer and interview style (use colons instead).

    Q: Did you go?
    A: Yes.

6. Do not use periods after items in a running summary.

    The rules: (1) punctuate properly, (2) write simply and (3) type neatly.

L. QUESTION MARK (?)

1. Use a question mark after a direct question.

May I go?

2. Use a question mark within parentheses to indicate a gap or uncertainty.

It was on (?) that I saw him. It was on April 13 (?) that I saw him.

3. In multiple questions, generally use a single question mark at the end of the question. But separate question marks may be used after each element for emphasis.

What are your summer plans—to paint, travel or simply relax? (Alternatively: *What are your summer plans? To paint? To travel? Or simply to relax?)*

4. Do not use a question mark with indirect or rhetorical questions.

May I suggest you try the filet. Why don't we go.

M. QUOTATION MARKS (" ")

1. Quotation marks are often overused. Routine phrases should not be quoted.

2. Use quotation marks around:

a. Direct quotations of sentences and paragraphs:

b. Key words and fragmentary quotations or to show emphasis or a shift in the level of speech:

He called her a "spy." The chairman said affairs at the Pentagon were in "a hell of a state."

c. Titles of books, essays, articles, plays, operas, movies, songs, paintings, statues, television programs and comic strips:

"The Naked and the Dead," "Our Town," "Aïda," "The Godfather," "Mr. Bojangles,"

Michelangelo's *"David," "All in the Family,"* *"Peanuts"*

NOTE: Do not use quotation marks in names of periodicals and references *(The Washington Post, Congressional Quarterly)* or in generic and numerical names of musical compositions *(Beethoven's Fifth Symphony* but *Beethoven's "Eroica" symphony).* (See 3b.)

d. Nicknames used with a surname (but do not use quotation marks in subsequent references and use parentheses if the nickname is inserted in the proper name):

"Jimmy the Greek" Snyder, Jimmy the Greek, Thomas (Tip) O'Neill Jr.

e. Misnomers and ironic references:

The "mansion" was a three-room cottage.
"Slim" weighed 230 pounds.

f. Slang and jargon not readily understood:

The train was "deadheaded."

g. Words or phrases being introduced and defined:

The term "gentlemen's agreement" is misused.
"Leading" means spacing between lines.

h. Potentially confusing terms, particularly in headlines:

Two Killed in "Queen Elizabeth" Accident

i. Coined words unless they have come into general use:

"cinemactor"

j. Clarifications:

He said "and," not "an."

3. Do not use quotation marks around:

a. Names of characters in books, plays, TV programs, operas, etc.:

He played Archie in "All in the Family."

b. Names of newspapers, magazines, periodicals and standard reference works:

The Washington Post, New West magazine, Congressional Quarterly, Who's Who, Jane's All the World's Aircraft

c. Question-and-answer and interview dialogue:

Q: When did you leave?
A: Late in September.

d. Names of pets, ships, plants, teams, special events, etc.:

his dog Zip, USS Forrestal, Houston Astros, Inaugural Day

e. Accepted colloquialisms:

brought in a wildcat well

f. The words *yes* and *no* in tallies:

13 voted yes and 12 no

g. Musical, legal and other technical terms derived from foreign languages:

andante movement, nol pros

h. Texts of documents and statements printed as separate entities.

4. Take care in relating the use of quotation marks to typographical considerations.

a. Use regular quotation marks in stories and captions but single quotation marks in headlines and subheads.

b. In quotes-within-quotes, alternate regular and single quotation marks.

c. In verse and extended quotations, use opening marks at the start of each stanza or paragraph and closing marks at the end of the last one.

d. Do not use quotation marks if another typographical device (such as italics or indented margins) is used.

N. SEMICOLON (;)

1. Semicolons should be used sparingly. Periods are usually better in a news story.
2. Use a semicolon:
   a. To indicate a close relationship between two elements of a sentence or two independent clauses:
      Peace is indivisible; if one country is menaced, all are menaced.
   b. To divide elements that need separation more emphatic than that provided by a comma:
      It is so in war; it is so in economic life; it cannot be otherwise in religion.
   c. To separate phrases containing commas or parentheses so as to avoid confusion:
      He demonstrated Model H1, which the committee liked best; Model G3, now outdated; and Model G23, a small unit unsuited to current needs.
   d. In lists of names and titles where commas alone would not make for clarity:
      Present were John Black, the mayor; Mary White, his accountant; and Peter Jones, his driver.
   e. In headlines where a period would be used in body type:
      13 Killed in Train Wreck; Loose Rail Blamed

O. SEQUENCE OF PUNCTUATION

1. Periods and commas always go inside quotation marks (both regular and single) whether they are part of the quotation or not.
   He called him "a snob." " . . . a snob," as he called him.

2. Colons and semicolons go outside quotation marks.

   Three projects were lumped under "Operation Blast": fission, fusion and atomic breeding. That ended the "emergency"; the plant reopened.

3. Question marks and exclamation points go inside or outside quotation marks depending on whether they apply to the quotation or to the statement including the quotation.

   "You're out!" the umpire shouted. "Oh, am I?" the batter retorted. What is the meaning of "snollygoster"?

4. Periods go inside or outside parentheses and brackets depending on whether the interpolated statement stands alone or is part of a complete sentence.

   He acted fast. (There's no time like the present.) There's no time like the present (or so he thought).

SPELLING

In general: Webster's New World Dictionary of the American Language *is The Post's authority for spelling. For words not found in* Webster's New World, *the authority is* Webster's Third New International Dictionary. Webster's New World *lists variant spellings jointly if usage "is about evenly divided between them," but adds that "in no case is the first spelling considered 'more correct.'" Variants are placed at the end of an entry if usage is less frequent.* Webster's Third *uses a different system. When variants are joined by* or, *they are coequal and usually listed in simple alphabetical order.*

When they are joined by also, *the first is more widely used. When a variant is preceded by* usu, *that is the usual and hence preferred spelling. When variants are coequal, The Post style is generally to use the shorter, newer or American spelling.*

A. SHORT FORMS AND LONG FORMS
Generally use short forms rather than long forms if both are acceptable:

> *ax, amid, among, amok, anoint, employe, furor, intern, mama, smolder, toward* (but *cigarette, demagogue, goodbye, synagogue)*

1. Short words derived from longer words need no apostrophe.
   > *copter, chute*
2. Do not use unaccepted or radically altered short forms except in proper names.
   > *silhouette,* not *silhouet; through,* not *thru (*but *New York Thruway)*

B. SEX DISTINCTIONS
Avoid sex distinctions in spelling; use the shorter form for both men and women.

> *alumnus, alumni, blond, brunet, confidant, fiance, protege*

C. DIPHTHONGS
Use *e* instead of the diphthongs *ae* or *oe* when the spellings are coequal.

> *archeology (*but *subpoena)*

D. *ER* AND *RE* ENDINGS
When either is acceptable use *er* rather than *re* endings.

> *caliber, saber, specter, theater, center (*but *Capital Centre* and *Ford's Theatre)*

E. SUFFIXES

Suffixes often change the spelling of a word, but there are so many rules and exceptions that the best practice is to consult *Webster's New World*. Some common rules:

1. One-syllable words ending in two consonants: unchanged when adding a suffix.

    fallen, singer

2. One-syllable words ending in vowel-plus-consonant: double the consonant if the suffix begins with a vowel.

    baggage, spotted (but *spotless*)

3. One-syllable words ending in two-vowel-plus-consonant: unchanged.

    aired, coolest, zealous

4. Multisyllabic words ending in two consonants: unchanged.

    crestfallen, unfolded

5. Multisyllabic words ending in vowel-plus-consonant, with primary stress on last syllable: double the consonant if the suffix begins with a vowel.

    abetting, beginner

6. Multisyllabic words ending in vowel-plus-consonant, with secondary stress on last syllable: varies widely.

    cataloguing, handicapping

7. Multisyllabic words ending in vowel-plus-consonant with no stress on last syllable: unchanged.

    bargaining, callously, solidly

8. Words ending in silent consonant: unchanged.

    crocheted, hurrahing

9. Words ending in silent *e*: drop the *e* before a suffix beginning with a vowel.

    completed, completing; livable, sizable

10. Words ending in vowel-plus-*e*: drop the *e* before suffixes beginning with *a* and *e*.
    arguable, bluest, issued
11. Words ending in consonant-plus-*y*: change the *y* to *i* unless the suffix begins with *i*.
    defiant, defying
12. Words ending in vowel-plus-*y*: unchanged.
    conveyance, graying
13. Words ending in vowel (except *e*) or *y* when adding a suffix beginning with a consonant: unchanged.
    photostat, radiogram
14. Verbs ending with a vowel (except *e*) or *y*, when adding a suffix beginning with a vowel: unchanged.
    alibied, alibiing, shanghaiing, tattooed
15. Words ending in *ce* or *ge*: keep the *e* only if the suffix begins with *a* or *o*.
    advantageous, changeable
16. If at all doubtful, check the spelling of words ending in *ise*, *ize* and *yze*.

F. PLURALS

Plurals also are subject to many rules and exceptions.

1. Most plurals are formed by adding *s*.
2. Nouns ending in *s, z, x, ch* and *sh* add *es*.
   buses, buzzes, dashes, foxes, torches
3. Nouns ending in consonant-plus-*y* change the *y* to *i* and add *es* (except proper names).
   armies, skies (but *Germanys*)
4. Nouns ending in vowel-plus-*y* add *s* (except those ending in *quy*).
   attorneys, chimneys (but *soliloquies*)
5. Nouns ending in vowel-plus-*o* add *s*.
   cameos, trios

6. Nouns ending in consonant-plus-*o* may add either *s* or *es*.

   egos, pianos, twos (but *echoes, heroes, tomatoes*)
7. Words borrowed from foreign languages often have two plurals.
   a. The English form is generally preferred.

      beaus, cellos, cherubs, chateaus, cactuses, formulas
   b. The foreign form is preferred if in common usage.

      criteria, data, media
   c. The foreign form is often preferred in scientific usage.

      algae, amoebae, larvae, nuclei
   d. Note that different spellings can have different meanings.

      antennas (aerials) but *antennae* (feelers);

      mediums (spiritualists) but *media* (the written and electronic press)
8. Compounds.
   a. In noun-adjective compounds, the noun is customarily pluralized.

      courts martial, heirs apparent, knights-errant
   b. But some such compounds are construed as a single word and the adjective is pluralized.

      attorney generals, battle royals, notary publics, poet laureates, sergeant majors
   c. In three-word compounds consisting of a noun and a prepositional phrase, the noun is usually pluralized.

      brothers-in-law, grants-in-aid, rights-of-way
9. Plurals of proper names take s or es.

   the John Joneses, the John Smiths
10. Consult *Webster's New World* on such forms as *passersby* and *cupfuls*.

11. Plurals of the names of animals vary widely; consult *Webster's New World.*

G. I-BEFORE-E RULE

Follow the *i-* before *-e* rule in words pronounced with an *ee* sound. That is, generally spell the word with *ie* (rather than *ei*) except after *c*:

> *believe, wield,* but *conceive, deceive*

1. Exceptions to this rule include *seize, leisure, neither, weird.*

2. Words pronounced with the *eye* or long *a* sound are generally spelled with *ei* (rather than *ie*).

> *heist, deign*

H. LOCAL NAMES

The following local names are often misspelled:

> *Allegany County* (Md.), *Alleghany County* (Va.), *Allegheny Mountains*
>
> *Arthur Capper Homes*
>
> *Beach Drive* (Rock Creek Park), *Beech Street* (in Washington and several suburbs)
>
> *Beall Avenue* (Rockville)
>
> *Belair Road* and *Belair* development (Bowie), *Belleaire Road* (Alexandria), *Bel Air* (county seat of Maryland's Harford County)
>
> *Belle Haven Boulevard* (Fairfax County), *Belleview Avenue* (Hyattsville), *Belleview Road* (McLean), *Belleview Boulevard* (Alexandria), *Bellevue Street* (Washington)
>
> *Bells Mill Road* (Montgomery County)
>
> *Beverley Hills* and *Beverley Drive* (Alexandria)
>
> *Brookings Institution*—not *Institute*

Brookville (Fairfax County), *Brookeville*
(Montgomery County), *Brookville Road* to
Brookeville, Md.
Bradlee Shopping Center (Alexandria), *Bradley
Boulevard* (Bethesda)
Capital Beltway
Capital Centre
East, North and South Capitol streets
(Washington)
Capital View (Prince George's County), *Capitol
View* (Fairfax and Montgomery counties)
Centreville (Va.)
Children's Hospital (Washington)
Culpeper (Va.)—not *Culpepper*
Dolley Madison Drive (McLean)
Dunn Loring (Fairfax County)
Dupont Circle (Washington)
Edsall Road (Fairfax County)—not *Edsel*
Fairmount Heights (Md.) but nearby *Fairmont
Heights High School*
Fort Lesley J. McNair (Washington)
Freedmen's Hospital (Washington)
Glenarden, Glenn Dale (Prince George's County)
Harford County (Md.)—not *Hartford*
Jay Street NE (named for *John Jay*)—not *J
Street*
Kamp Washington (Fairfax County)
Lorcom Lane (Arlington)
National Institutes of Health—not *Institute*
Oxon Hill (Md.)
Smithsonian Institution—not *Institute*
St. Elizabeths Hospital (Washington)
Veirs Mill Road (Montgomery County)—not
Viers

I. TRADE NAMES

The following trade names are often misspelled:
Chesapeake & Ohio Railroad, E. I. du Pont de Nemours & Co. (or Du Pont Co.), Encyclopaedia Britannica, Karmann Ghia, K mart, Lions Club, Penn Central Railroad, Reader's Digest, Scot Tissue, 7-Eleven, Thom McAn, Volkswagen. (Airlines generally is one word, but Delta, Eastern, Japan, Ozark, United and Western all use *Air Lines*; and it is *Trans World Airlines* and *Pan American World Airways*.)

J. FOREIGN NAMES

Foreign spellings present special problems. Characters and sounds in one language may have no equivalent in English. Spellings may vary within a language. Usage may vary from culture to culture. The rules that follow are necessarily general.

1. Lowercase articles, prepositions and conjunctions (*de, di, du, la, le, von,* etc.) when used with a full name. Capitalize when used without the first name.
   Charles de Gaulle, De Gaulle
2. Accent marks in Latin and Germanic languages should be used if the paper can set such characters in type. If not, ignore foreign accent marks except for the German vowel-with-umlaut, which should appear as vowel-plus-e.
   Guenther Grass
3. The Arabic *al, an* and *ash* should be eliminated in a person's name, but capitalized (without a hyphen) in newspapers' names.
   Ahmed Hassan (al) *Bakr; Al Ahram*
4. The Arabic guttural sound *qaf* takes a *q* rather than

qu or *k*, and the *ee* at the end of a name takes *i* rather than *y*.

Qaddafi, Ali Sabri

5. In Chinese names, do not capitalize the name following the hyphen.

Premier Hua Kuo-feng

6. In Russian names, spell the ending *sky* rather than *ski* and *ov* rather than *off* (but continue using familiar forms even if incorrect).

Malinovsky, Sovorrov (but *Rachmaninoff* rather than *Rakhmaninov*)

7. In Russian women's names, do not use the feminine ending unless the woman has a reputation independent of her husband's.

Nina Khrushchev (not *Khrushcheva*) but
Yekaterina Alekseyevna Furtseva, former Soviet minister of culture and wife of Nikolai Firyubin

8. Preferred spellings of names of certain foreign cities are:

Algiers, Antioch, Antwerp, Archangel, Athens, Baghdad, Bangkok, Basel, Bayreuth, Beirut, Belgrade, Bern, Brunswick, Bucharest, Cape Town, Coblenz, Cologne, Copenhagen, Corfu, Dunkerque, Florence, Frankfurt, Genoa, Goteborg, The Hague, Hamelin, Hanover, Hong Kong, Jakarta, Jeddah, Katmandu, Khartoum, Kingston (Jamaica), *Kingstown, Kompong Som* (formerly *Sihanoukville*), *Kurile, Leghorn, Lisbon, Lod, Lyons, Marseilles, Mogadishu, Monterrey* (Mexico), *Mukden, Munich, Naples, North Cape, Nuremberg, Peking, Phnom Penh, Prague, Riyadh, Rome, Saint John* (New Brunswick), *St. John's* (Newfoundland), *Salonika, Sanaa, Sofia, Taipei, Tehran, Tiflis, Tokyo, Turin, Valetta, Warsaw, Wiesbaden*

9. Preferred spellings of names of certain foreign countries are:

   Bahrain, Cameroon, Congo (former French colony, not to be confused with *Zaire,* the former Belgian Congo), *Gambia, Lebanon (no the), Madagascar* or *Malagasy Republic, Mozambique, Namibia, the Netherlands, North Yemen, the Philippines, Qatar, Romania, South Yemen, Sudan (no the), Sri Lanka, Trinidad-Tobago, United Arab Emirates (Abu Dhabi, Dubai, Sharjah, Ajman, Ras al Khaimah, Fujairah, Um al Qaiwain), Zaire*

10. Preferred spellings of certain foreign places are:

    Taiwan Strait, Gulf of Riga, Mt. Sinai, Pescadores, Rhodes, Mt. Vesuvius, Zuider Zee

K. FREQUENT MISSPELLINGS

The following words and phrases are often misspelled (an asterisk indicates the preferred Post spelling):

aberration, abscess, abysmal, a cappella, accommodate, accompanist, acknowledgment, adrenaline, adviser, affidavit, a la carte, align, all right, all-round (not all-around), already, amok, analyze, annulment, annulled, anoint, apparatus, asinine, assassinate, attorneys, ax*

baby-sit, bailiff, ballistics, balloon, barbecue, barbiturate, bar mitzvah, bas-relief, beige, beneficent, benefit, berserk, besiege, bettor, bivouac, bivouacking, blase, blond (both genders), B'nai B'rith, brunet (both genders)

caffeine, caldron, calendar, caliber*, calorie, canister, caramel, Caribbean, catalogue,

catsup, cesarean*, chaise longue*, chandelier,
chauffeur, chaperon, chili, cigarette, cliché,
cloture, clue, coed*, cognizance, Colombia*
(South America), *colossal, connoisseur,
consensus, consistency, cookie, corduroy,
corollary, coup d'etat, crystallize, cupfuls, czar**

*dachshund, daffodil, daiquiri, debilitate, deify,
deity, deluxe, demagogue, derring-do, despise,
diaphragm, diarrhea, diesel, dietitian,
diphtheria, discernible, dissension, doughnut,
drought, drunkenness, duffel bag, dumbbell,
dumbfounded**

earnest, ecstasy, eerie, embarrass, employe, en
masse, en route, euchre, excel, exhilarate, exhort,
exorbitant, extol, extravagant, exuberant, eying**

fiber, fiery, finagle, fluorescent, fluoridate,
forfeit, free lance* (n.), *free-lance* (adj., v.), *frieze,
fuchsia, fulfil*, furor, fuselage, fusillade*

gabardine, gaiety, garnishee, gelatin, glamor,
glycerin, goodbye, goodwill, gorilla, gray*,
grievance, grievous, gruesome, guerrilla, gypsy*

*habeas corpus, Halloween, hara-kiri, harass,
harebrained, heinous, hemorrhage, hemorrhoids,
hiccup, hors d'oeuvres*

*imminent, impasse, impostor, impresario,
incandescent, infrared, innocuous, innuendo,
inoculate, installment*, iridescent, irrelevant*

judgment, jujitsu, jukebox

kerosene*, khaki, kimono, klieg light*

labyrinth, lacquer, lambaste, languor, larynx,
legionnaire, liaison, libel, likable, lilies, liquefy,
lissome, liter*, livable, lovable*

maitre d'hotel, marijuana, massacre, medieval,
mediocre, memoranda, mileage, minuscule,
mischievous, missile, misspell, moccasin, more
or less, mustache*

naive, naivete, naphtha, nauseous, negligee,
New Year's Day, numbskull*

*obbligato, obeisance, objets d'art, oculist,
offense, okay, old-timer, omniscient,
ophthalmologist, outrageous*

*pantomime, papier-mache, paraffin, parallel,
paraphernalia, pari-mutuel, part-time (adj.),
pasteurize, pastime, pavilion, penicillin, percent,
percentage, peripatetic, persevere, personnel,
pharmaceutical, phenomenon, phlegm,
picnicking, pinochle, pique, plagiarism, plaque,
plebiscite, plow*, poignant, poinsettia,
Portuguese, potpourri, powwow, precipitant,
precursor, predominant, prerogative, propellant,
propeller, prurient, pummel, pygmy*

quarantine, questionnaire, queue

*raccoon, rarefied, raveling, receive, reciprocal,
reconnaissance, rehearsal, relevant, renaissance,
repellent, resistant, restaurateur, resuscitate,
reveille, rhapsody, rheumatism, rhubarb, rhyme,
rhythm, ricochet, rock 'n' roll, rumba*

*saber, saboteur, saccharin, sacrilegious,
salable, satellite, savior*, schizophrenia, seize,
separate, sequoia, sheik, shillelagh, siege, sieve,
silhouette, sizable, skeptic, skiing,
skulduggery*, slalom, sleigh, sleight of hand,
smolder*, somersault, souffle, souvenir, specter,
spiel, straightjacket, strategem, strenuous,
stylebook, subpoena, sulfur, supersede, surfeit,
surveillance, svelte, swastika, sycophant,
synagogue*, syphilis, syrup*

*table d'hote, taffeta, tantamount, tariff, tattoo,
teen-age, teen-ager, temblor, temperamental,
tentacles, terrazzo, till (not til), toboggan,
tonsillitis, toupee, traipse, tranquility*, T-shirt,
turbulent*

U-boat, ukulele, undersecretary, usable

*vacuum, vehement, vengeance, vermilion,
versatile, Veterans Day, vicissitude, vilify,
villain*

wash-and-wear, weird, welsh, welsh rarebit,
whisk, whodunit, wield, wiener, willful, woolly*

Xerox, X-ray (n., v., adj.)*

yacht, yield, yogurt*, Yom Kippur

zigzag, zinc, zinnia, zoology

XI   TIME ELEMENTS, DATELINES, ADDRESSES

In general: Time elements and place elements should tell a reader clearly when and where events in a story occurred and where the story was written. A given day should not appear as, say, today *in one story,* tomorrow *in another and* Friday *in a third. Cities should be identified by state or nation both in datelines and in general usage unless they are instantly recognizable without such identification. Addresses and place names unfamiliar to most readers should be followed by a point of reference.*

A. TIME ELEMENTS

1. Do not use a date in the "dateline"—the first line of a story, which normally includes city and state or country of origin and often includes a news agency logotype.

ABILENE, Tex. (AP)—A tornado roared
through downtown Abilene yesterday.

2. Designate days and dates as follows:

   a. For the current three days, use *today* (date of publication), *tomorrow* and *yesterday.*

   President Black is expected to announce the
   veto today. He told a press conference
   yesterday the bill is too costly. Congress will
   try tomorrow to override the veto.

   b. For the 11 other days in the current two weeks, use the name of the day, qualified by *next* or *last* if necessary.

   He will speak to the nation next Monday (not
   June 3).

   c. For the other days in the current two-year period, use the date or month alone, qualified by *next* or *last* if necessary.

   He signed the treaty on Oct. 13 (or last
   October, but not on Oct. 13, 1977 or in October
   1977 if the date is within the current
   two-year period.)

   d. In headlines, use *today* but not *tomorrow* or *yesterday*; use the name of the day instead.

   e. The week begins on Sunday. The preceding seven days constitute *last week*; the current Sunday and the following six days are *this week.* Stories in the Sunday paper often refer erroneously to *next week* when *this week* is meant.

   f. Use the most meaningful time terminology.

   He has been waiting for two weeks (not since
   March 7).

   g. *Midnight* refers to the end of the day, not the beginning of the day.

3. State time in local terms; then convert it to time for your zone if it is significant for the reader.

   The quake struck Los Angeles at 9 p.m. The

*president will speak from Los Angeles at 6 p.m.
(9 p.m. EST).*

4. Placement of the time element.
   a. Ordinarily time precedes day and day precedes
      place.
      *He will speak at noon Tuesday from the East
      Room.*
   b. The time element usually follows the verb or verb
      phrase but may precede the verb to avoid an
      awkward construction.
      *President Black said yesterday he will veto the
      bill. President Black yesterday called the
      defeat of his omnibus health bill tragic.*
5. In writing a specific date, abbreviate the month; in
   month-and-year references, do not use abbreviations
   or commas.
   *Feb. 15, 1965, from February 1965 through
   September 1968*
6. It's *noon* and *midnight*, not *12 noon* and *12 midnight*;
   and it's *6 p.m. today* or *6 o'clock tonight*, not *6 p.m.
   tonight.*
7. It's *30 B.C.* but *A.D. 30.*
8. The federal fiscal year runs from Oct. 1 through
   Sept. 30. *Fiscal 1980* is the year ending Sept. 30,
   1980. Do not use the abbreviation *FY* except in such
   specialized copy as texts, tables and the Federal
   Diary.

B. DATELINES

1. Datelines generally may be used only if the reporter
   was present in the city on the day mentioned and if
   the reporter provided most of the information in the
   story. (Merely telephoning sources in another city
   does not justify use of that city as the dateline.)
2. If the reporter must leave a city before filing a story,

as often happens during a war or a political campaign, he or she may still use the city as the dateline and file from the next convenient point.

3. Stories with no time element (such as a feature, background or trend story) may carry a dateline even if later written elsewhere, provided that the reporter gathered most of the information in the city and was there within a week of the publication date.

4. Roundup stories generally carry no dateline. But if the roundup focuses on a single city and the reporter is writing from there, a dateline may be used.

5. In datelined stories, material from another city and another source should generally be enclosed in brackets. In stories without datelines, such material should generally be included with credit but without brackets. (See IX J.)

6. Post staffers should not use datelines on stories originating in metropolitan Washington—the District of Columbia, the cities of Alexandria, Fairfax, Falls Church and Rockville and the counties of Arlington, Fairfax, Loudoun, Montgomery, Prince George's and Prince William.

7. Use artificial and temporary datelines sparingly.
    a. Stories from the United Nations enclave in New York carry the dateline UNITED NATIONS—(no state).
    b. Ships at sea may be used as datelines but military bases should not be used unless they are a separate geographical entity.
        ABOARD THE USS KENNEDY OFF GIBRALTAR: FORT RILEY, Kan.; but not *FORT HOLABIRD,* which is in Baltimore.
    c. Use *CAPE CANAVERAL* (no state) instead of *KENNEDY SPACE CENTER* and *HOUSTON* instead of *JOHNSON SPACE CENTER.*

8. The names of many states may be abbreviated in datelines (see list in VI F) but American territories, Canadian provinces and foreign countries should not be abbreviated (except for the U.S.S.R.).

9. In sports events occuring in suburbs of or communities within metropolitan areas, use the more specific locality in the dateline if it has an established identity of its own.

   WIMBLEDON, England: FOREST HILLS, N.Y.; HIALEAH, Fla.; ARLINGTON, Tex.

10. The following American cities need not be identified by state in either datelines or ordinary usage:

Albuquerque	Houston	Omaha
Anchorage	Indianapolis	Philadelphia
Atlanta	Iowa City	Phoenix
Baltimore	Jacksonville	Pittsburgh
Birmingham	Jersey City	Richmond
Boston	Las Vegas	Roanoke
Buffalo	Los Angeles	Salt Lake City
Charlottesville	Louisville	San Antonio
Chicago	Memphis	San Diego
Cincinnati	Miami	San Francisco
Cleveland	Miami Beach	San Jose
Colorado	Milwaukee	Seattle
Springs	Minneapolis	St. Louis
Dallas	Nashville	Toledo
Denver	Newark	Tucson
Des Moines	Norfolk	Tulsa
Detroit	New Orleans	Williamsburg
El Paso	New York	
Fort Worth	Oakland	
Hollywood	Oklahoma	
Honolulu	City	

11. The following foreign cities need not be identified by nation in either datelines or ordinary usage:

Algiers	The Hague	Peking
Amsterdam	Hamburg	Phnom Penh
Ankara	Hanoi	Prague
Athens	Havana	Quebec City
Bangkok	Helsinki	Rio de Janeiro
Barcelona	Hong Kong	Rome
Belfast	Istanbul	Rotterdam
Belgrade	Jakarta	Saigon
Beirut	Jerusalem	San Salvador
Bombay	Johannesburg	Seoul
Bonn	Kiev	Shanghai
Bordeaux	Leningrad	Singapore
Brasilia	Lisbon	Stockholm
Brussels	London	Sydney
Bucharest	Luxembourg	Tehran
Budapest	Madrid	Tel Aviv
Buenos Aires	Manila	Tokyo
Cairo	Marseilles	Toronto
Calcutta	Melbourne	Tunis
Canton	Mexico City	Vancouver
Copenhagen	Milan	Vatican City
Dublin	Montreal	Venice
East Berlin	Moscow	Vienna
Edinburgh	Munich	Warsaw
Florence	Nanking	West Berlin
Frankfurt	Naples	Winnipeg
Geneva	New Delhi	Yokohama
Genoa	Oslo	Zurich
Glasgow	Ottawa	
Guatemala City	Panama City	
	Paris	

C. ADDRESSES

1. The correct form is *1150 15th St. NW.*
2. North, East and South Capitol streets and the Mall

divide the District of Columbia into quadrants: Southeast, Southwest, Northeast, Northwest. The full width of the three "Capitol" streets is not in any quadrant but addresses along them are in one or another. Hence an auto accident may occur at *15th and East Capitol streets* (with no quadrant designation) but a dwelling is located at *1501 East Capitol St. NE.* Do not abbreviate the quadrant streets. It is *North Capitol street*, not *N. Capitol street*.

3. References to neighborhoods are often useful, particularly in the context of community action or concern. But the story should mention the nearest main intersection or a familiar landmark as well.

4. In crime stories and others in which publication of a precise address could bring harm, embarrassment or harassment to an innocent person, list the address in this style: *the 200 block of I Street NE* or *an upper Connecticut Avenue restaurant.*

5. Some Washington area streets and locales sound like others. See X H for distinctions and correct spellings.

6. Many area addresses have post offices different from the political jurisdiction in which they are located. When in doubt, check; it may be critical in a police or court story.

DESKWORK: EDITING, HEADLINES, BYLINES, CAPTIONS, TYPOGRAPHY XII

In general: Though newspaper technology is changing rapidly, the editing process is not. This chapter deals with creative and judgmental aspects of editing that hold true regardless what production system is used, and with technical and typographical aspects of editing for a large metropolitan paper.

A. THE EDITING STAFF

1. The Post has a news staff of about 400 persons. About half are reporters. The other half are photographers, editorial writers, artists, librarians, researchers, news aides, copy aides, dictationists—and editors.

The news staff is headed by the executive editor, managing editor and deputy managing editor. The editorial and opposite-editorial ("op-ed") pages are headed by the editorial page editor and a deputy.

2. An assistant managing editor heads each news department—financial, foreign, metro, national, Outlook/Book World, The Magazine/Weekend/TV Channels, photo/graphics, sports and Style—and the news desk, which coordinates production of the entire paper.

3. Most departments have assignment or originating editors who plan advance coverage, assign reporters, maintain contact with them during the day, and review the completed stories for general content.

4. Some stories are sent back to the reporter for additional information or clarification or to be rewritten. But most go on to the department's copy editors, headed by a copy-desk chief or slot editor, who fine-tune stories, write headlines and captions and examine each edition for errors that creep in.

5. The display of stories and photos is determined by news editors after consultation with originating editors about the contents and merits of their stories. The pages are assembled in the composing room by a printer, following the news editor's layout with the help of a makeup editor.

6. The Post staff includes a number of special editors— such as the travel, fashion, food, real estate and design editors—who write stories about their fields, assign and edit stories by outside writers and supervise production of their sections.

B. COPY EDITING

1. Copy editors are a newspaper's last line of defense against error. They must challenge every fact or statement that seems doubtful.

2. Copy editors are also responsible for ensuring that a story is comprehensible to the ordinary reader. What may be clear to the writer or originating editor may be murky to the copy editor and unintelligible to the reader. They look at each word, phrase and sentence to see if the thought can be stated more clearly or in fewer words or if the word, phrase or sentence is needed at all. But in making substantive changes, they check with the originating editor or reporter to ensure that the change is correct.

3. Copy editors are guardians of style and taste. They should make copy conform to style, and challenge lapses in taste. But they do not change copy just because they would have written it differently. Writing styles vary—as they should.

4. The copy desks are a vital link between the newsroom and the composing room. Good deskwork can help ensure a quick, smooth closing; poor deskwork can cause confusion and loss of time. Copy editors should ensure that copy is legible, that it is properly marked, that all necessary instructions are on it, that "takes" or pages are properly numbered and that markers are clear and complete. Above all, copy editors and slot editors must promptly inform the news editors or makeup editors when changes or problems arise.

5. See Figure 3 on Page 168 for examples of copy-editing symbols.

C. HEADLINES

1. Headlines are a newspaper's showcase. A good headline can lure a reader into a story. A poor one can drive the reader away. Some guidelines:

   a. Build the headline around key words—the "must" elements of the story. Ignore unnecessary elements and use the space for fresh ones.

FIGURE 3—Copy Editing Symbols

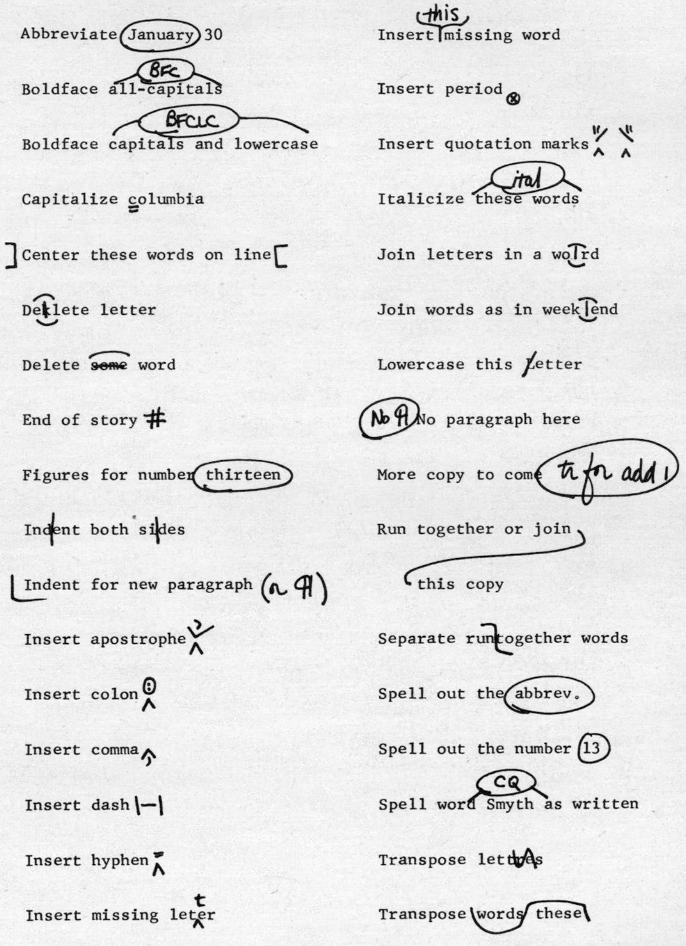

Abbreviate (January) 30

Boldface all-capitals (BFC)

Boldface capitals and lowercase (BFCLC)

Capitalize columbia

] Center these words on line [

Delete letter

Delete some word

End of story #

Figures for number (thirteen)

Indent both sides

Indent for new paragraph (¶)

Insert apostrophe

Insert colon

Insert comma

Insert dash |—|

Insert hyphen

Insert missing letter (t)

Insert this missing word

Insert period ⊗

Insert quotation marks

Italicize these words (ital)

Join letters in a word

Join words as in week end

Lowercase this letter

No ¶ No paragraph here

More copy to come (tr fr add 1)

Run together or join this copy

Separate run together words

Spell out the (abbrev.)

Spell out the number (13)

Spell word Smyth as written (CQ)

Transpose letters

Transpose (words these)

ADEQUATE   *Mayor to Ask Tax Increase*
           To Balance City's '77 Budget
BETTER   *Mayor to Ask Tax Increase*
           On Incomes, Food, Liquor

b. Use an action verb and preferably the active voice.

ADEQUATE   *Tax Plan Is Hit by Council*
BETTER   *Council Assails Tax Plan*

c. Be specific.

POOR   *Message Stirs Controversy*
BETTER   *Tax Warning Splits Senate*

d. Avoid weak and hackneyed words (*county, area, slaps, hikes*).

e. Do not use names, terms, places, initials or other references not instantly understandable to the reader.

POOR   *Throckmorton Named to RYA Board*
BETTER   *N.Y. Banker Named to Youth Board*

f. Headlines generally should have a subject and verb. Label headlines (without a verb, such as *A Town Without Remorse*) are acceptable on features and soft-news stories. But verb headlines (without a subject, such as *Calls Mayor Crackpot*) are not acceptable.

g. Avoid awkward breaks of thoughts or elements.

Smith Runs Dead
Last For Mayor

h. The use of *said* or *says* requires a second verb. Avoid this kind of construction.

Driver Said Blameless
In Beltway Crash

i. Use the present tense unless references to the past or future make it awkward.

NO   *34 Die in Traffic Last Year*
YES   *34 Died in Traffic Last Year*

    j. Do not repeat words in a headline or bank.

    k. Do not end the first line of a headline with an adjective, preposition, article or conjunction.

    l. Headlines should almost fill each line (except for centered headlines).

2. Rules governing the use of abbreviations, capitalization, numerals and punctuation in headlines are covered in Chapters VI through X.

3. Headline counts.

    a. The following table is a reliable guide for counting headlines in Bodoni bold roman:

        $1/2$ unit—f, i, j, l, t; all punctuation; space; numeral 1.

        1 unit—a, b, c, d, e, g, h, k, n, o, p, q, r, s, u, v, x, y, z; capitals I and J; all numerals except 1.

        $1^1/2$ units—m, w; all capitals except I and J.

        2 units—capital M and W.

    b. To determine the maximum count of a Bodoni bold roman or italic headline, see Figure 4 on Page 171. Bodoni light permits a slightly higher count.

D. BYLINES AND CREDIT LINES

1. Bylines identify the writer to the reader, help establish reporters in their beats and with their sources, and give writers both credit and responsibility for their work. But bylines should be used only when, in the desk's judgment, credit is deserved; they should not be used on routine stories, rewrites of handouts or pickups from other news media.

2. A reporter may have more than one byline in the paper or even on the same page. On sidebar stories, a signature is often preferable to a byline.

3. Use a writer's preferred byline as it appears on the

FIGURE 4—Headline Counts

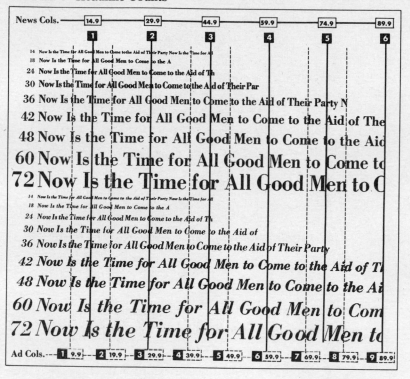

byline list distributed periodically to copy desks. Don't use *John Black* one day, *John J. Black* the next and *Jack Black* a third day.

4. If a double byline does not fit on one line of type, the *and* goes on the second line.

> **By John Black**
> **and Mary White**
> Washington Post Staff Writers

5. Follow these styles for bylines:

a. Domestic news stories, with or without dateline.

By John Black
Washington Post Staff Writer

b. Story by a staffer permanently stationed abroad.

By Mary White
Washington Post Foreign Service

c. Story by a domestic staffer traveling abroad.

By John Black
Washington Post Staff Writer

d. Datelined domestic staff story with no byline.

By a Washington Post Staff Writer

e. Datelined foreign staff story with no byline.

Washington Post Foreign Service

f. Domestic or foreign story by a stringer.

Special to The Washington Post

g. Stringer story with no byline.

Special to The Washington Post

h. Story by a senior editor of The Post or other publication.

By John Black
Executive Editor, The Washington Post

By Mary White
Executive Editor, The Boston Globe

i. Story by AP or UPI, bylined with no dateline.

By John Black
Associated Press

j. Story by AP or UPI without byline or dateline.

United Press International

k. Story by AP or UPI, bylined and datelined.

> **By Mary White**
> Associated Press

l. Story by AP or UPI, datelined with no byline.

> **MINNEAPOLIS (UPI)—A downtown bank . . .**

m. All other stories by a single paper or agency.

> **By John Black**
> Reuter
>
> Christian Science Monitor

n. Copyright lines (upon request).

> **By Mary White**
> ©1977, The Los Angeles Times

o. Stories compiled from wire service copy (used at the beginning of story).

> From news services

p. Roundup columns taken largely from wire copy without substantial rewriting (used at the end of a story).

> From news services and staff reports

q. Stories reported by three or more persons, where only one or two get a byline (used at the end of a story).

> *Also contributing to this story were staff writers John Black and Mary White and researcher Henry Jones.*

r. Signatures on "Letters from . . . " and occasional sidebars (flush right at the end of a story).

> **—JOHN JONES**

s. Stylized bylines are used in several sections including Style, the editorial and op-ed pages, Book World and the Weekly sections. They usually are set in 12-point Bodoni bold italics with no agate line.

t. Stories based largely on staff reporting but including copy from other sources are treated as staff-written. Other sources may be credited within the story *(". . . ," Associated Press reported.)* Or a longer section might be appended to a staff-written story with an italic credit.

> *United Press International reported*
> *from Beirut:*

E. PICTURES, ARTWORK AND CAPTIONS

1. Assignments.

   a. Most assignments for pictures, maps, sketches and other artwork originate with reporters and their editors and are meant to go with specific stories. The photo and graphics departments execute the assignment, usually with a staff photographer or artist but often with a stringer, free lancer, wire service or other outside source.

   b. Photo assignment forms at The Post are completed in triplicate—one copy for the originating desk, one for the photographer and one for the photo desk.

   c. In making photo assignments, reporters or their editors must:

   (1) Describe the story in enough detail that the photographer knows what kind of pictures will illustrate it.

   (2) Include all essential information, such as names, correct addresses, specific road directions, phone numbers, required dress, required credentials, deadlines and the kind of pictures desired (head shots, action, casuals, file art, a layout, etc.).

   (3) Clear the picture with the subject, particularly if photographers must enter a school, prison, hospital or private business premises or photograph a child or an ailing or controversial person.

(4) Give the photo department enough time to handle the assignment (it may take hours to take and print a suburban photo and several days to get one from another state).

d. In making graphics assignments, reporters and editors should follow the same guidelines as for photos but should also tell the artist and mapmakers what information is to be included and what is irrelevant.

2. Kinds of captions.

a. After news editors receive pictures and artwork from the photo and graphics department, they choose the artwork to be used, crop it, send it on for retouching and engraving and give the copy desk a caption form with detailed instructions for the copy editor and typesetter (Figure 5, Page 176).

b. The "stand-alone" (s/a) caption has no accompanying story and must be complete. It usually has a boldface lead-in but sometimes will take a headline instead. Some page one captions will "key" to inside stories; the last words should be *See story on Page —*.

BLACK'S NEW HOME—Former president Black and his wife Mary plan to move into this house in the Rancho Granada section of Palm Springs, Calif., in a few days. They have leased the house, which comes with a new swimming pool and a spectacular view.

c. The "with-story" (w/s) caption accompanies a story and usually is just a single line. If more than one line is needed to explain the picture, copy editors should notify the news editors promptly.

HEW Secretary White takes the oath of office.

d. W/s head-shot pictures of individuals usually take

FIGURE 5—Caption Form

SLUG *BLACK*		With Story	Stand Alone	(Lead in Headline)	Special Instructions

Edition	Department	Type Style	Measure — All Lines 6 pt. Indent Each Side.	
(Capital**)	(News) (N) F / L Ar	(News Black Face—8 on 10 bold)	**News Columns**	**Ad Columns**
Late City***	Sports	8 pt. BOLD CAPS	1 col. 14.9 pi.	1 col. 9.9 pi.
	Women's	8 pt. Bold Clo	(2 col. 29.9 pi.)	2 col. 19.9 pi.
Replate	Sunday	10 pt. bold roman	3 col. 21.10 pi. double up	3 col. 29.9 pi.
			4 col. 29.4 pi. double up	4 col. 19.4 pi. double up
Final	Financial	*12 pt. bold italics*	5 col. 24.3 pi. triple up	5 col. 24.4 pi. double up
		12 pt. lite italics	6 col. 29.3 pi. triple up	6 col. 29.4 pi. double up
Early Run	Theaters	Other	One Line Centered	7 col. 22.7 pi. triple up
				8 col. 25.11 pi. triple up
				9 col. 29.3 pi. triple up

Agate Credit *Associated Press*   Your Initials *RW*

xxxxxxxxxxxxxxxxxxxxxxxxxxxxxxxxxxxxxxxxxxxxxxxxxxxxxxxxxxxxxxxxxxxxxxxxxxxxxxxxxxxxx

Column headers (vertical): 1 ad column · 1 news column · 2 & 4 ad columns · 3 news columns · 7 ad columns · 5 news columns / 5 ad columns · 8 ad columns · 2, 4 & 6 news columns / 3, 6 & 9 ad columns

BLACK'S NEW HOME -- Former President Black and his
wife Mary plan to move into this home in the Rancho
Granada section of Palm Springs, Calif., in a few
days. They have leased the house, which comes with
a swimming pool and a spectacular view of the desert.

view.

The measures above are gauged for News Black
Face 8 on 10 pt. bold using a Pica typewriter

Note: Double up captions must fill 4, 6 or 8 typewritten
lines to insure balance. Tripled up lines take 6, 9, 12, etc.

two lines: a centered nameline and a centered ellipsis line that brings out an important element about the story. (One-column obituary captions use only the nameline.)

PRESIDENT BLACK
. . .third straight defeat

 e. The "extended" caption is really a brief story set in special measure. No further caption is needed.

3. Writing captions.

 a. Captions must be accurate and complete. Enough information usually is found in carbons of a story, in the wirephoto caption or on the photographer's caption sheet attached to the photo. If more information is needed, ask for additional wire copy or check with the reporters or assigning editor. If information is still too sketchy, consult the news desk so that the photographer or wire service can be contacted or the picture killed.

 b. Photographers and caption writers should identify everyone appearing prominently in the picture, and point out interesting or important details that the reader might miss. But do not labor the obvious.

 c. Use the form "from left," not "left to right." Again, do not labor the obvious if the picture includes, for example, the president, the vice president and a Japanese official.

 d. Use the present tense to describe action in progress in the picture. But avoid such awkward constructions as *John Black heads out to sea yesterday.*

 e. Keep such details as traffic death tolls out of the caption so that it does not have to be updated.

 f. If a past event is pictured, the caption should say so, giving the date or year when possible. Old head shots should have an agate line saying *19— photo.*

g. Copy editors should be careful not to include in the caption a person or detail that has been cropped out.

h. With multicolumn head shots, do not state merely that, for example, *President Jones appears before newsman.* Use a quote or detail to make it interesting, such as *President Jones: Ready for a showdown.*

i. The caption may be dropped for special effect or when the photo (or map or chart) itself contains an identifying legend.

j. Avoid such weak usage as *John Jones is shown* . . . ; use the space to say something interesting.

4. Photo and art credit lines.

a. Almost all photos and artwork require agate credit lines. The only exceptions:

(1) One-column or similar head shots.

(2) Certain pieces where a credit is impractical or undesirable, such as routed cuts, drop-in drawings, copies of magazine covers, photos off a TV screen, uncredited file photos that cannot be traced, etc.

b. The credit line should name the person or agency that produced the photo or artwork and indicate the role of The Post, if any. For example:

(1) Staff photos (including those taken by reporters, editors, news aides and copy aides).

By Mary White—The Washington Post

Photos by John Black—The Washington Post

(2) Stringer and special photos made at The Post's request (even if transmitted by AP or UPI).

By Mary White for The Washington Post

CBS for The Washington Post

(3) Free-lance and off-the-street photos.

By John Black

(4) Wire service photos taken at The Post's request.

By Associated Press for The Washington Post

(5) AP or UPI photos provided routinely or requested from their files.

Associated Press

United Press International

(6) Wire service photos from other sources.

Hsinhua via UPI
White House photo via AP

(7) Photos from other news sources and references.

Chicago Sun-Times
Bettmann Archive
By John Black—Magnum
Sovfoto
Library of Congress
NASA
Freer Gallery
Bethlehem Steel
United Auto Workers

(8) Copyrighted photos.

© 1977,The New York Daily News

c. Credit lines for maps, charts, diagrams, drawings and other artwork should follow these styles:

(1) By staff artists.

By John Black—The Washington Post
Montage by Mary White—The Washington Post
Photos by John Black, design by Mary White—The Washington Post

(2) By staff artists based largely on other sources.

The Washington Post from NASA diagram

(3) By stringers or free lancers even if signed.

By John Black for The Washington Post

(4) One-column or similar maps and charts.

The Washington Post

(5) From other news agencies and reference sources.

By Mary White—The Los Angeles Times
Encyclopaedia Britannica

d. The graphics department will provide correct credits for all photos and artwork that pass through its hands. But each desk and department is responsible for crediting other pieces and for seeing that credit lines are correct as they appear in the paper.

F. MISCELLANEOUS TYPOGRAPHIC DEVICES

1. *Keys* are references on a section front page to a story inside the section. They are written in brief headline style and set in italic type. The page number is set flush right.

*President unveils details of his tax
cut program.* *Page A23.*

2. *Precedes* are editorial notes or explanations preceding a story. They are written in prose style and set in italic type.

*The writer has just returned from a
three-day tour of the battle zone.*

3. *Quotation precedes* are quotations used at the start of a story. They are set in italic and take an Ionic agate credit line set flush right.

*"We began the ascent with the
warning still ringing in our ears."*
—Guide John Black

4. *Shirttails* are devices within a story to provide a transition or at the end of a story to provide additional credit. They are set in italic.

*Washington Post staff writer John
Black reported from Beirut:*

*Also contributing to this report was
researcher Mary White.*

5. *Dots* or *bullets* are used sparingly to itemize matter instead of using figures. Do not use dashes.

> • A five- or six-month period during which interstate pipelines could buy gas on an emergency basis outside the regular price controls.
> • Emergency authority for the president to order pipeline companies to transfer gas among themselves.
> • Telephone hotlines in state and federal energy offices to help critically short users find fuel supplies.

6. *Three-em dashes* and *dingbats* are used between sections of long stories to indicate abrupt changes in time or locale or the end of an anecdote.

> . . . resting his chin on his hands, leaning on the handle of a cane, looking a little tired.
>
> ———
>
> A few weeks ago I had the occasion to be in New York, and when I got off the Metroliner under the Garden, I went up to his restaurant.

7. Italic and boldface type may be used within text for emphasis, to designate foreign words and for typographic effect. Those faces should generally not be used for word definitions or for titles of publications and works of art, despite such use in this volume.

G. TYPOGRAPHY

1. Type size and width is measured in points and picas.

1 point   = $1/72$ inch.
12 points = 1 pica.
6 picas   = 1 inch.

NOTE: 13.9 picas means 13 picas and 9 points, not 13 and $9/10$ picas.

2. Indention is measured in ems and ens (also known as M's and N's or muts and nuts). Strictly speaking, an em is the square of any point size and an en is half that; in 10-point type, an em is 10 points and an en 5 points. But when referring to indention, a "pica em" is used. Thus:

   1 em = 12 points.
   1 en =   6 points.

3. Many newspapers are converting from hot-type composition (metals lines of type) to cold-type composition (paper paste-up type). Type faces vary from paper to paper. In hot type, The Post uses 8- and 9-point Corona for text, Ionic agate for credit lines, Spartan agate for tabular matter and Bodoni (14- through 84-point) for headlines. In cold type, it uses 9-point Crown for text, Doric agate for credit lines, Techno Book agate for tabular matter and Bodoni or KC Bodoni for headlines.

4. The Post and many other papers have converted to a *six-on-nine* page—a six-column news page superimposed on a nine-column ad page (Figure 6, Page 185). Because the formats are not entirely compatible, special sets (or measures) must often be ordered for stories, cuts and headlines. The following tables show the sets for filling both news columns and ad columns.

   a. Sets for ordinary news matter.

NEWS COLUMNS	SET (in picas)	AD COLUMNS	SET (in picas)
1	13.9	1	8.9
2	13.9	2	18.9 (1 leg)
3	13.9	3	13.9 (2 legs)
4	13.9	4	18.9 (2 legs)
5	13.9	5	15.5 (3 legs)

News Columns	Set (in picas)	Ad Columns	Set (in picas)
6	13.9	6	13.9 (4 legs)
		7	16.3 (4 legs)
		8	18.9 (4 legs)
		9	13.9 (6 legs)

b. Sets for boxes.

News Columns	Set (in picas)	Ad Columns	Set (in picas)
1	11.3	1	6.3
2	12.6 (2 legs)	2	16.3
3	12.11 (3 legs)	3	12.6 (2 legs)
	20.0 (2 legs)	4	17.3 (2 legs)
4	13.1 (4 legs)	5	16.10 (3 legs)
	17.11 (3 legs)	6	13.15 (4 legs)
5	13.3 (5 legs)		17.11 (3 legs)
	16.10 (4 legs)	7	15.7 (4 legs)
6	13.4 (6 legs)	8	14.3 (5 legs)
	16.3 (5 legs)	9	13.4 (6 legs)
			16.3 (5 legs)

c. Sets for headlines.

News Columns	Set (in picas)	Ad Columns	Set (in picas)
1	14.9	1	9.9
2	29.9	2	19.9
3	44.9	3	29.9
4	59.9	4	39.9
5	74.9	5	49.9
6	89.9	6	59.9
		7	69.9
		8	79.9
		9	89.9

d. Cut sizes.

NEWS COLUMNS	WIDTH (in picas)	AD COLUMNS	WIDTH (in picas)
1	13.9	1	8.9
2	28.9	2	18.9
3	43.9	3	28.9
4	58.9	4	38.9
5	73.9	5	48.9
6	88.9	6	58.9
		7	68.9
		8	78.9
		9	88.9

H. ESTIMATING STORY LENGTHS

1. One inch of 13.9-pica hot type equals:
- in 8 point, $4\frac{1}{2}$ wire copy lines or $5\frac{1}{2}$ typed lines.
- in 9 point, $3\frac{1}{2}$ wire copy lines or $4\frac{1}{2}$ typed lines.

2. To convert inches of 13.9 to inches of 15.5, multiply by .9; to 16.3, multiply by .85; to 18.9, multiply by .75.

3. Cold-type lengths are calculated by computer and displayed on the reporter's or editor's terminal.

FIGURE 6—Superimposed
News and Advertising Columns

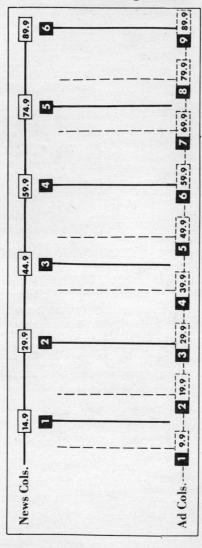

XIII

THE FEDERAL GOVERNMENT

A. *Executive branch*
B. *Legislative branch*
C. *Judicial branch*
D. *Regulatory agencies*

In general: Under the Constitution, the federal government consists simply of three coequal branches, each serving as a check and balance against the others to prevent abuses and to protect the public interest. In practice, however, it also includes an ever-changing labyrinth of administrations, agencies, boards, bureaus, commissions, committees, councils, courts, departments, offices and systems. They may be monstrous or minuscule, obvious or obscure, but together they take actions and make decisions affecting millions of lives and billions of dollars. A Washington press corps numbering in the thousands works to keep the public informed and the government responsive and honest.

A. THE EXECUTIVE BRANCH

1. The executive branch consists of the president and vice president (both elected for four-year terms),

their staffs, the Cabinet departments, various Cabinet-level advisory agencies and a number of independent agencies and commissions.

2. The president has the power to propose and veto legislation, grant pardons (except in impeachment cases) and make treaties (subject to Senate ratification) and "executive agreements" (binding but not subject to Senate ratification).

3. The vice president is president of the Senate and has no other constitutional duties. The 25th Amendment empowers the president to appoint a vice president when a vacancy occurs. It was first used in 1973 when Gerald Ford succeeded Spiro Agnew.

4. The Cabinet is not mentioned in the Constitution and no act of Congress created it. But the earliest presidents began gathering advisers and the Cabinet became an accepted part of the executive branch.

   a. The Department of Agriculture (established in 1889) promotes agriculture through divisions dealing with such matters as international commodity programs, conservation, animal and plant health inspection, marketing and consumer services, credit to farmers (Farmers Home Administration) and emergency relief (Rural Electrification Administration).

   b. The Department of Commerce (1913) promotes economic and technological development within the United States. Its duties also include promoting tourism, maintaining the U.S. merchant marine and aiding underdeveloped countries through research and grants.

   c. The Department of Defense (1949) is responsible for the military security of the United States and includes the three separate services—the

Army, the Navy and the Air Force. The department is by far the largest and is headed by the civilian secretary and the uniformed Joint Chiefs of Staff. Ultimate authority rests with the president as commander in chief of the armed forces.

d. The Department of Energy (1977) coordinates the government's energy pricing and development policies. Rates for sale of natural gas and electricity are set by a five-person regulatory board, housed within the department but independent of the secretary. Creation of the department consolidated most energy-related functions previously scattered among more than 50 other departments and independent agencies.

e. The Department of Health, Education and Welfare (1953) is the federal agency most involved with the daily lives of Americans. HEW's divisions include the Office of Human Development, the Office of Education, the Center for Disease Control, the Food and Drug Administration, the Health Resources Administration, the National Institutes of Health, the Social Security Administration, the Office for Civil Rights and the Alcohol, Drug Abuse and Mental Health Administration.

f. The Department of Housing and Urban Development (1965) administers programs and loans for housing and community development and ensures compliance with fair-housing laws.

g. The Department of the Interior (1849) is the nation's principal conservation agency. It monitors the use of public land (some 550 million acres) and operates manpower and youth training programs. Divisions within the agency are the National Park Service, the Bureau of Mines, the Geological Survey, the Bureau of Indian Affairs, the Bureau of Land Management, the Bureau of Outdoor Recreation, the Bureau of Reclamation and the Mining Enforcement and Safety Administration.

h. The Department of Justice (1870) is, in effect, the public's law firm. It includes the antitrust, civil, civil rights, criminal, land and natural resources and tax divisions. There are also five bureaus within the agency: the Federal Bureau of Investigation, the Bureau of Prisons, the U.S. Marshals Service, the Drug Enforcement Administration and the Law Enforcement Administration.

i. The Department of Labor (1913) administers more than 130 federal labor laws and oversees working conditions, pay, discrimination, unemployment insurance and workers compensation. Its Occupational Safety and Health Administration sets standards, issues citations and proposes penalties for noncompliance with safety standards. Its Bureau of Statistics maintains figures on employment.

j. The Department of State (1789) develops and carries out the nation's foreign policy. (In recent years its work has been augmented by the National Security Council, based in the White House.) The department includes the Foreign Service (the professional diplomatic corps and staff), the Agency for International Development (which provides economic and social aid to underdeveloped countries) and the Office of Protocol.

k. The Department of Transportation (1966) coordinates and administers transportation policy. It includes the Coast Guard, the Federal Aviation Administration, the Federal Highway Administration, the Federal Railroad Administration, the National Highway Traffic Safety Administration, the Urban Mass Transportation Administration, the St. Lawrence Seaway Development Corporation and the Materials Transportation Bureau.

l. The Department of the Treasury (1789) formulates and recommends tax and fiscal policies, serves as the nation's financial agency and manufactures coins and currency. Its divisions include the Customs Service, the Bureau of Engraving and Printing, the Internal Revenue Service, the Savings Bonds Division, the Secret Service, the Bureau of Alcohol, Tobacco and Firearms and the Federal Law Enforcement Training Center.

5. The president is served by a number of policy-making or advisory agencies in addition to the Cabinet departments.

   a. The Office of Management and the Budget (established in 1970) advises the president on budgetary matters, oversees expenditures within the executive branch, develops its own budget proposals and evaluates budget proposals from Congress. The OMB director must be confirmed by the Senate.

   b. The Council of Economic Advisers (1946) analyzes the economy and advises the president on economic policy. Its three members are appointed by the president and confirmed by the Senate.

   c. The National Security Council (1947) advises

the president on national security matters and analyzes policies of federal agencies dealing with national security. Its members are the president, the vice president, the secretaries of State and Defense and the NSC executive director (who is a presidential adviser).

d. The Central Intelligence Agency (1947) collects and produces intelligence on foreign affairs, advises the president and the National Security Council and conducts overt and covert operations abroad. The director and deputy director are appointed by the president and confirmed by the Senate.

e. The Council on Environmental Quality (1969) develops and advises the president on national environmental policies and helps the president prepare the annual environmental quality report to Congress. The council's three members are appointed by the president and confirmed by the Senate.

f. The Council on Wage and Price Stability (1974) monitors key economic indicators, such as wages, costs, productivity, profits and prices. It also reviews the work of other agencies and the impact of their programs on inflation.

6. Independent Agencies.

a. ACTION (1971) is the umbrella organization for such volunteer agencies as the Peace Corps (foreign) and VISTA (domestic), which teach methods of social and technological self-help in undeveloped areas abroad and to the disadvantaged in the United States.

b. The Administrative Conference of the United States (1964) provides a forum in which government agency heads discuss and evaluate federal programs. The conference has 10 members appointed by the president for three-year terms and a chairman appointed by the president for a five-year term.

c. The Board for International Broadcasting (1973) oversees the operations of Radio Liberty (which broadcasts to the Soviet Union) and Radio Free Europe (which broadcasts to Poland, Czechoslovakia, Hungary, Romania and Bulgaria). The board's five members are appointed by the president for three-year terms.

d. The Commission on Civil Rights (1964) encourages the development of equal opportunity practices in both government and the private sector but has no enforcement authority.

e. The Community Services Administration (1974) is the successor agency to the Office of Economic Opportunity. It develops programs to aid the poor.

f. The Environmental Protection Agency (1970) is the principal government agency responsible for environmental control, pollution research and the preparation of environmental impact statements.

g. The Equal Employment Opportunity Commission (1965) is responsible for ending discrimination in government employment and promoting equality in private sector employment.

h. The Export-Import Bank (1934) can borrow money from the U.S. Treasury to finance and facilitate exports and imports. Its main programs involve direct credits to borrowers outside the United States, export credit insurance for American businesses and export credit guarantees.

i. The Federal Aviation Agency (1958) regulates air commerce, controls navigable air space, develops aids to navigation and communications and promulgates safety regulations and air traffic rules.

j. The Farm Credit Administration (1933) supervises activities of federal land banks and federal land bank associations. It is designed to provide adequate and dependable credit for agricultures.

k. The Federal Deposit Insurance Corporation (1933) was established after banks failed during the Depression. The FDIC protects and insures bank deposits. Its board of directors includes the comptroller of the currency and two members appointed by the president for six-year terms.

l. The Federal Election Commission (1974) monitors federal campaigns for compliance with the 1974 Campaign Finance Act and distributes federal funds for presidential campaigns.

m. The Federal Mediation and Conciliation Service (1947) provides mediators in labor disputes. It may be invited by either party or intervene on its own, but it has no enforcement authority.

n. The Federal Reserve System (1913) is the nation's central bank. The Fed profoundly affects the national economy through its power to control money and credit. Its board of governors has seven members appointed by the president for 14-year terms.

o. The General Services Administration (1949) is the country's supply and office-space agency. It distributes all office materials and forms used by federal employees, leases space for federal offices, distributes funds for presidential transitions and maintains the National Archives.

p. The Indian Claims Commission (1946) hears and decides claims against the government by Indian tribes.

q. The National Aeronautics and Space Administration (1958) is the principal federal agency dealing with space exploration and research.

r. The National Credit Union Administration (1970) charters, insures, supervises and audits federal credit unions.

s. The National Endowment for the Arts (1965) encourages and supports cultural advancement.

t. The National Labor Relations Board (1935) administers labor relations law. It has investigatory and civil prosecutory powers but can act in unfair labor practice cases only when formally requested to do so by an employer or a union.

u. The National Mediation Board (1934) provides railroads and airlines with an avenue for adjustment or labor-management disputes.

v. The National Science Foundation (1950) provides federal assistance for research and education in all areas of science.

w. The National Transportation Safety Board (1975) investigates major transportation accidents and recommends preventive actions to federal agencies and the transportation industry. The board has five members appointed by the president for five-year terms.

x. The Overseas Private Investment Corporation (1969) encourages and assists private American investment in developing countries. Its 11-member board includes six from the private sector and five from the federal government.

y. The Pension Benefit Guaranty Corporation (1974) guarantees basic pension benefits if pension policies default. Its board of directors consists of the secretaries of Labor, Commerce and the Treasury. A seven-member advisory board (two from labor, two from business, three from the public) is appointed by the president.

z. The Selective Service System (1941) conducted the military draft until it ended in 1973. It now is responsible for planning and training programs in the event more persons are needed for military service than the current voluntary program provides.

aa. The Small Business Administration (1953) is the principal federal agency concerned with aiding and lending money to small businesses.

bb. The Civil Service Commission (1883) administers a merit system of federal employment. More and more federal jobs are coming under commission jurisdiction rather than being subject to patronage or political appointment.

cc. The United States Information Agency (1953) is the principal propaganda machine for the United States and can operate only abroad. It has geographic divisions and four media: the Voice of America, the Information Center Service, the Motion Picture and Television Service and the Press and Publications Service.

dd. The United States Postal Service (1970) is responsible for mail delivery and is the only federal agency whose employment policies are governed by collective bargaining. Before 1970 the U.S. Post Office was a Cabinet agency run by a postmaster general.

ee. The Veterans Administration (1930) deals with veterans benefits, compensation, pensions and loans. It also maintains hospitals, outpatient clinics and nursing homes for veterans.

B. THE LEGISLATIVE BRANCH (CONGRESS)
1. The Senate.
   a. The Senate is composed of 100 members, two from each state, who are elected by popular vote for six-year terms. One-third of the Senate is elected every two years. A senator must be at least 30 years of age and a resident of the state from which he or she is elected, and must have been a United States citizen for at least nine years.
   b. The vice president of the United States is the presiding officer of the Senate; in his or her absence the duties are taken over by a president pro tempore elected by that body. Highly important in conducting Senate business are the majority and minority leaders and their "whips," who are responsible for enforcing party discipline and ensuring attendance. The leaders are elected in party caucuses at the start of each Congress and appoint their own whips. The majority leader seeks to achieve party goals through the legislative system. The minority leader, who usually does not attempt to secure

major legislation, is basically limited to organizing opposition to majority bills.

2. The House of Representatives.

   a. The House is currently composed of 435 members. The number representing each state is determined by its population, but every state is entitled to at least one representative. Members are elected by popular vote for two-year terms. A representative must be at least 25 years old and a resident of the state from which he or she is elected, and must have been a U.S. citizen for seven years.

   b. The only House officer formally elected is the Speaker (a title that dates from 1377 in England's House of Commons). As the presiding officer, the Speaker decides points of order, refers bills and resolutions to committees, appoints members of select (special) committees and votes in case of a tie on the floor. As in the Senate, the House majority and minority leaders are chosen at party caucuses at the beginning of each Congress. The majority leader formulates the party's legislative program in cooperation with the Speaker and steers the program through the House. The minority leader's role is similar in structure but different in content: to present the minority view on pending legislation. It is also a more tenuous and frustrating position, and minority leaders often retire or are removed. The party whips are appointed by their leaders and in turn select as many as 18 assistant whips.

3. Sessions.

   Section 4 of the Constitution requires that "Congress shall meet once every year." In 1933 the 20th Amendment established that each Congress convenes on Jan. 3 of each odd-numbered year and ends on Jan. 3 of the next odd-numbered year. Each Congress has two regular sessions (the second beginning on January 3rd of even-numbered years) and each session is supposed to adjourn by July 31.

4. Powers of Congress.

   a. The fiscal powers of Congress have long been considered the most important. Granted to the Congress by various articles of the Constitution, these powers include not only assessing and collecting taxes, but also coining money and regulating interstate and foreign commerce.

   b. In addition, Congress has the power to establish post offices and post roads; establish courts inferior to the Supreme Court; declare war; raise and maintain an army and navy; and "make all laws which shall be necessary and proper for carrying into execution the foregoing powers, and all other powers vested by this Constitution in the Government of the United States. . . . "

   c. Congress also has the power to propose amendments to the Constitution whenever two-thirds of both houses find it necessary. Proposed amendments become effective when ratified by the legislatures or special conventions of three-fourths of the states. (If two-thirds of the state legislatures demand changes in the Constitution, Congress must call a constitutional convention.)

d. Under the Constitution, the Senate is granted certain powers not granted to the House. The Senate approves or disapproves certain presidential appointments by majority vote, and treaties must be approved of by a two-thirds vote. Both houses act in impeachment proceedings, which may be instituted against the president, the vice president and all civil officers of the United States. The House has sole power of impeachment (indictment) and the Senate has the sole power to try impeachments.

5. Enactment of laws.

a. To become law, a bill or resolution must be passed by both the House and the Senate and must be signed by the president or passed over the president's veto by a two-thirds vote of both houses. (If the president does not act within 10 days, the bill automatically becomes law— unless Congress is not in session.)

b. The work of preparing and considering legislation is conducted largely by committees. Both houses have a number of standing committees as well as select (special) committees for closer study of particular legislation. There also are joint committees composed of members of both houses. Members of the standing committees are chosen by vote of the entire body. Members of all other committees are appointed by the presiding officers. Each bill and resolution is referred to the appropriate committee, which may report it out in its original form, vote it down in committee, make changes in it or allow it to die without action.

C. THE JUDICIAL BRANCH

1. Creation and authority.

   a. Article III, Section 1 of the Constitution provides that "the judicial power of the United States shall be vested in one Supreme Court, and in such inferior courts as Congress may from time to time ordain and establish." The Supreme Court was created in accordance with this provision and by the authority of the Judiciary Act of September 24, 1789.

   b. The Constitution also provides that "the judges, both of the Supreme and inferior courts, shall hold their offices during good behavior," indicating that all judgeships are virtually lifetime appointments.

   c. Although the power to appoint federal judges resides in the president, the power to create judgeships and to establish their salaries resides in Congress.

2. Organization.

   a. The Supreme Court.

   (1) The Supreme Court consists of the chief justice and eight associate justices. The president nominates the justices; confirmation is by Senate Judiciary Committee approval and an affirmative floor vote in the Senate. A clerk, reporter of decisions, marshal and librarian are appointed by the court.

   (2) The Supreme Court term begins, by law, on the first Monday in October of each year and continues as long as business before the

court requires, usually until about the end of June. Six members constitute a quorum. Approximately 4,000 cases are passed upon in the course of each term. Only members of the court bar may practice before it.

(3) The Constitution states that "in all cases affecting ambassadors and other public ministers and consuls, and those in which a state shall be party, the Supreme Court shall have original jurisdiction. In all other cases . . . the Supreme Court shall have appellate jurisdiction" (i.e., is limited to review of lower-court decisions). Whether the court accepts a case for review depends on whether the decision from the inferior court presents questions or conflicts important enough or of such a constitutional nature as to warrant the court's consideration.

b. The United States courts of appeals.

(1) The courts of appeals are intermediate appellate courts created to relieve the Supreme Court of considering all appeals in federal cases. The decisions of the courts of appeals are final except insofar as they are subject to discretionary review by, or direct appeal to, the Supreme Court.

(2) The United States is divided into 11 judicial circuits, each with a U.S. court of appeals. At present each circuit has from three to 15 permanent judgeships, and each circuit is assigned a Supreme Court justice.

c. The United States district courts.

The district courts are the trial courts for cases

within general federal jurisdiction. Each state and the District of Columbia and Puerto Rico has at least one district court, and some larger states have as many as four. Cases from the district courts are reviewed by the appropriate United States court of appeals, except for injunctions by special three-judge district courts, certain decisions holding acts of Congress unconstitutional and certain criminal decisions appealed directly to the Supreme Court.

d. Special courts.

(1) The Temporary Emergency Court of Appeals has exclusive jurisdiction over all appeals from district courts in cases arising under the economic stabilization laws. It consists of eight district and circuit judges appointed by the chief justice.

(2) The U.S. Court of Claims has original jurisdiction to render judgment in the case of any claim against the United States founded upon the Constitution, any act of Congress, any regulation of an executive department, or any express or implied contract, and for liquidated and unliquidated damages in cases which do not involve torts (wrongful actions). The jurisdiction of the court is nationwide. Trials are conducted wherever most convenient for the claimant and his witnesses. The court is staffed by 15 trial judges.

(3) The U.S. Court of Customs and Patent Appeals was created to decide questions arising under the customs laws and was later given jurisdiction to review certain patent and trademark cases. The court consists of a chief judge and four associate judges.

(4) The U.S. Customs Court has exclusive jurisdiction over civil actions arising under the tariff laws and over civil actions brought by American manufacturers, producers or wholesalers. The court is composed of a chief judge and eight associate judges. Its principal office is in New York, but it can hear cases at any port of entry.

(5) Territorial courts have been established by Congress in Guam, Puerto Rico, the Virgin Islands and in the Canal Zone. Except in Puerto Rico these courts have jurisdiction over many local matters ordinarily decided in state courts. The district court of Puerto Rico is classified like other district courts. The territorial judges serve eight-year terms.

(6) The U.S. Military Court of Appeals is the final appellate tribunal for court-martial convictions. There is no further direct review. The court consists of three civilian judges appointed by the president.

(7) The U.S. Tax Court tries and adjudicates controversies involving tax deficiencies or overpayments. All cases except small ones are subject to review by the U.S. court of appeals. The court is in Washington, but cases are tried wherever convenient to taxpayers. The court is composed of 16 judges but each case is tried by only one.

D. REGULATORY AGENCIES

Congress has delegated various regulatory functions to independent regulatory agencies. Members are appointed to fixed terms by the president, but no political party may have more than a one-member majority on the agency's presiding body.

1. The Civil Aeronautics Board (established in 1938) promotes and regulates the economic aspects of the civil air transport industry within the United States and between the United States and foreign countries. It grants licenses and approves fares and agreements involving air carriers.

2. The Commodity Futures Trading Commission (1974) regulates futures trading to prevent price manipulation, market corners and the dissemination of false commodity and market information.

3. The Consumer Product Safety Commission (1972) seeks to protect the public against unreasonable risks from consumer products, to develop uniform safety standards for consumer products and to promote research into the causes and prevention of product-related deaths, illnesses and injuries. The commission can ban hazardous products.

4. The Federal Communications Commission (1934) regulates telephone and telegraph carriers, allocates radio frequencies, licenses radio and television stations, monitors broadcasts and administers international communications treaties.

5. The Federal Maritime Commission (1961) regulates the foreign and domestic waterborne offshore commerce of the United States. It is authorized to maintain surveillance over fair trade rates and issue licenses in accordance with shipping statutes.

6. The Federal Trade Commission (created in 1914 as an administrative agency, made independent in 1951) is charged with preventing practices leading to monopoly, such as unfair competition and false advertising, and with keeping the free enterprise system from being corrupted or stifled. It can investigate and bring suit against offenders.

7. The Interstate Commerce Commission (1887) fixes rates, sets standards for reasonable service, issues permits, controls consolidations and mergers of carriers and regulates safety devices and standards for railroads, motor carriers, certain domestic water carriers and pipelines and freight forwarders.

8. The Nuclear Regulatory Commission (1975) is responsible for ensuring that civilian use of nuclear materials and facilities is consistent with public health, safety, environmental quality, national security and antitrust laws. It issues licenses and establishes regulations for the construction and use of nuclear electricity-generating facilities.

9. The Securities and Exchange Commission (1934) provides the public with information and protection in the securities and financial markets. It regulates the issuance of securities, supervises stock exchanges and regulates holding and investment companies. The commission has power to compel disclosure, to prevent fraud in the purchase and sale of securities, to obtain court orders, to revoke the registrations of brokers and to prosecute persons who violate federal securities laws.

XIV LOCAL GOVERNMENT

A. *The metropolis*
B. *District of Columbia*
C. *Maryland*
D. *Virginia*
E. *Regional agencies*

In general: The demographic and political complexity of metropolitan Washington gives The Washington Post a unique readership and vastly complicates news coverage of local government.

A. THE METROPOLIS
1. A demographic profile.
   a. Metropolitan Washington is not just another huge urban complex. It is a city of the world, the national capital, a political mecca . . . a center of law, communications, finance, culture, history, tourism, research and scholarship . . . the scene of many of America's grandest and most squalid

events . . . the hub of the East Coast megalopolis
. . . a place where fortunes can be made . . .
above all, a symbol and showcase of the nation.

b. Washington is America's northernmost southern
city, one of its largest black-governed cities and
the home of its most stable black middle class and
some of its most wretched poor.

c. Its surburban population as a whole is among the
wealthiest, best educated, most traveled and most
sophisticated in the world.

d. It has a large, ever-shifting transient population—foreign diplomats, businesspeople on temporary assignment, rotating military families,
short-term government aides—and consequently
a newspaper readership that includes many new-
comers and non-natives eager to learn about their
new home.

2. Community organization.

a. In most metropolises, satellite cities (county
seats, college towns, agricultural centers) have
become the prime instruments of local government—the Fort Lauderdales, Ann Arbors, Boul-
ders and Long Beaches. But in surburban Washington, most important business is conducted by
four huge counties—Prince George's (694,000),
Montgomery (585,000), Fairfax (543,000) and Arlington (149,000). Aside from the cities of Alexandria (107,000) and Rockville (49,000), large
communities exist in name only. Bethesda (90,-
000) lists just two public agencies in the telephone book—the fire department and the rescue
squad. Wheaton (83,000) lists none.

b. The communities that do have self-government
are for the most part small and scattered—such

as Falls Church (10,000) and Herndon (9,500) in Virginia, Kensington (2,000) in Montgomery and 28 separate municipalities in Prince George's.

3. News coverage of the area.

   a. It is not by accident, then, that there is no significant daily paper in the Washington suburbs. The communities big enough to support a daily have no power or cohesiveness; the communities that do have power and cohesiveness are too small to support one.

   b. Moreover, the Capital Beltway circling through the Washington suburbs gives the area a community of interest rare among American metropolises. It is not unusual for a Washingtonian to live in one jurisdiction, work in a second, shop in a third and spend leisure time in a fourth.

   c. But far from making comprehensive local coverage easier, the Washington metropolitan structure makes it almost impossible:

   • The counties are immense. Montgomery sprawls over 507 square miles. It is 40 miles from one end of Fairfax to the other.

   • The populations are huge. Except for Washington itself, Prince George's is the largest jurisdiction—city or county—south of Baltimore and east of the Mississippi. Montgomery and Fairfax are not far behind.

   • The county bureaucracies are complicated. The telephone book has almost four columns of Fairfax County government listings, including 60 separate agencies.

   • In addition, there are hundreds of local civic, social, recreational, cultural and special-interest groups. The "new town" of Reston had at last count some 50 organizations that could be sources of legitimate local news from time to time.

- At the other extreme is the great web of regional, interjurisdictional, metropolitan, state and federal agencies that govern the Washington area—from the Metropolitan Washington Council of Governments to the National Park Service.
- Nor is the end in sight. The Council of Governments notes that "most recent state and federal legislation places considerable emphasis on metropolitan areas as the basic planning units."

B. DISTRICT OF COLUMBIA

1. City government.
   a. Residents of Washington (the District of Columbia) are governing themselves for the first time in more than 100 years. In 1874 Congress repealed an earlier and limited form of home rule, and from then until 1967 the city was governed by Congress and three presidentially appointed commissioners. Pressure for home rule was blocked by southern congressional forces repeatedly after World War II, but in 1967 President Johnson used his reorganization authority to replace the three commissioners with a single commissioner (mayor) and a nine-member council—all appointed, yet more representative of the city. In 1973, Congress approved home rule; in 1974, it was approved by referendum; and on Jan. 2, 1975, it became fact.
   b. Under home rule, Washington citizens elect a mayor and a 13-member City Council. The council chairman and four other members are elected

at large (no more than three from any one political party). All officials serve four-year terms—the mayor and chairman concurrently and the other 12 council members on a staggered basis.

c. The city government has most traditional municipal powers, but Congress must approve its budget and can exercise additional control through its annual federal appropriation for the city. The mayor can veto council action; the council can override the veto by a two-thirds vote; but the president can uphold the mayoral veto. In addition, Congress can veto legislation within 30 days after the mayor signs it and can legislate for the city at any time. The president appoints local judges from nominations made by a local legal commission. He may also assume emergency police powers. Finally, federal buildings, monuments and parklands are part of a federal enclave separate from city jurisdiction.

2. Courts.

a. The Court Reorganization Act of 1970 created a judicial system for the District of Columbia comparable to a state court system. Under it the D.C. Superior Court assumed the duties of the former General Sessions, Juvenile, Tax and Domestic Relations courts and was given the responsibility for trying all felony, criminal and civil cases previously tried by the U.S. District Court.

b. The act also made the D.C. Court of Appeals comparable to a state court of appeals. It handles appeals of cases tried in Superior Court. Appeals from the D.C. Court of Appeals go directly to the U.S. Supreme Court.

c. The strengthening of the two D.C. courts enabled the federal courts there to resume their intended duties as arbiters of disputes involving governmental agencies and triers of federal crimes. Appeals of cases tried by the U.S. District Court are taken to the U.S. Court of Appeals.

3. Federal representation.
   a. District residents have voted for president and vice president since 1961, when the 23rd Amendment empowered them to choose three electors.
   b. The District is not represented in the Senate but does elect a House delegate who serves a two-year term and enjoys all congressional privileges except voting on the House floor.
   c. The Senate and House both have District of Columbia committees which originate legislation dealing with the city.
4. Schools.
   a. Washington's school board was appointed by U.S. District Court judges until 1967, when Congress empowered the District to elect an 11-member board. Members serve four-year staggered terms.
   b. The school board sets policy for the system, hires the school superintendent and approves the annual budget before it is presented to the mayor, City Council and Congress. Six regional superintendents administer the system and report to the superintendent.
   c. Washington has two public colleges. Three separate institutions—Washington Technical Institute, Federal City College and D.C. Teachers College—were combined into the University of the District of Columbia, a land-grant school, in 1977. The fourth—Gallaudet College—was established by Congress to serve the deaf and has its own board of trustees.
   d. Washington has six major private colleges:

American University, Catholic University, Georgetown University, George Washington University, Howard University and Trinity College.

C. MARYLAND
1. State government.
   a. Maryland's elected state officials are a governor, a lieutenant governor, a comptroller of the treasury and an attorney general. They and members of the state legislature and most county officials are elected to four-year terms in even-numbered nonpresidential-election years. The governor may be elected to only two consecutive terms. There is no limit on the others.
   b. The General Assembly (legislature) consists of the 47-member Senate and the 141-member House of Delegates. One senator and three delegates are elected from each of the 47 legislative districts. The legislature meets in Annapolis for 90 days every year starting the second Wednesday in January.
2. Courts.
   a. The lowest state court is the district court, which handles most minor criminal, traffic and civil matters and may conduct preliminary hearings in felony cases. Its judges are appointed to 10-year terms by the governor, subject to confirmation by the State Senate.
   b. The circuit court handles trials of the more serious criminal and civil cases. Its judges are appointed by the governor and stand for election to 15-year terms at the next general election.
   c. The Court of Special Appeals hears appeals in most civil and criminal cases. Its judges are

elected for 15-year terms, and the governor designates one of them as chief judge.

d. The Court of Appeals is the state's highest court. Its seven judges are elected for 15-year terms and the governor designates one as chief judge.

3. Federal representation.

In addition to its two senators, Maryland has eight representatives, three of whom represent districts in the Washington area. The 8th District includes all of Montgomery County except a rural slice of the northern county and a few precincts in Takoma Park near the District line. The 5th District covers those Takoma Park precincts plus northern and central Prince George's County. The 4th District consists of southern Prince George's and all of Anne Arundel County.

4. Schools.

a. The county governments in Maryland and Baltimore city run their own school systems, financed largely through state aid and local property taxes. In many rural counties, school board members are appointed by the governor, although there is a clear trend toward elected school boards such as those in Montgomery and Prince George's.

b. The University of Maryland, with its main campus in the Prince George's town of College Park, is the main state center of higher education. In addition, the state runs a number of four-year colleges, including one in Bowie, and two-year community colleges, including one in Montgomery County and one in Prince George's County.

5. Local government.

Maryland is divided into 23 counties and the city of Baltimore. Except for Baltimore, county government is dominant in the state.

6. Suburban Washington.

    a. Both Prince George's and Montgomery have strong county executive forms of government. In each county, the executive is elected by voters every four years and has strong control over day-to-day operations of county government. Montgomery has a seven-member council; Prince George's has an 11-member council. In both counties, the councils confirm most major appointments by executive, vote on legislation and have exclusive final responsibility for zoning.

    b. Both Prince George's and Montgomery have many municipalities. They often have their own police forces, trash collection and snow removal operations.

    c. Montgomery has a seven-member school board elected for four-year terms. Prince George's school board terms vary from three to seven years.

D. VIRGINIA

1. State government.

    a. Virginia's three elected state officials—governor, lieutenant governor and attorney general—serve four-year terms. The governor cannot succeed himself, but the others can do so.

    b. The Virginia General Assembly consists of a 100-member House of Delegates, elected every two years, and a 40-member State Senate, elected every four years.

2. Courts.

    a. The state's three-tiered judicial system is composed of general district (local) courts, circuit courts and the nine-member State Supreme Court. Judges are elected by the General Assembly, but the governor fills vacancies when the assembly is not in session.

b. The U.S. district attorney's office for the Eastern District of Virginia is located in Alexandria, where a federal court sits regularly.

c. The 4th Circuit Court of Appeals sits in Richmond and hears cases on appeal from federal courts in the states of Virginia, Maryland, West Virginia, South Carolina and North Carolina. A three-member State Corporation Commission appointed by the General Assembly regulates business activities and sets utility rates.

3. Federal representation.

In addition to its two U.S. senators, Virginia has 10 representatives—two of whom come from Northern Virginia. The 10th District is composed of Arlington County, northern Fairfax County, Loudoun County, Fairfax City and the city of Falls Church. The 8th District is composed of the city of Alexandria, southern Fairfax County, Prince William County and the northern tip of Stafford County.

4. Schools.

a. Generally each Virginia county and city has an independent school system, financed largely from state aid and local property taxes. School boards are appointed by the local county boards or city councils in Northern Virginia. They run the schools and submit budgets to their local governing bodies, but have no taxing authority.

b. Among the state's largest universities are the University of Virginia in Charlottesville, Virginia Polytechnic Institute and State University (VPI or Virginia Tech) in Blacksburg, Old Dominion University in Norfolk and Virginia Commonwealth University in Richmond. The only university in Northern Virginia is George Mason University in Fairfax County and is part of the state university system. Marymount College, a Catholic girls' school, is located in Arlington. Northern Virginia Community College with five separate campuses is part of a statewide system of two-year colleges.

5. Local government.
Virginia has 95 counties, 38 independent cities and scores of towns dependent on their parent counties.

6. Suburban Washington.
   a. In all Northern Virginia jurisdictions, the chief administrator is appointed and serves at the pleasure of the jurisdiction's legislative body. Those bodies are elected and hold the real power locally; they make policy, legislate, approve budgets and set tax rates. But home rule is limited in Virginia, and local jurisdictions must obtain General Assembly approval before acting in many matters.
   b. Alexandria: It is an independent city with its own seven-member city council (including the elected mayor), appointed city manager, court system and police force.
   c. Arlington County: A five-member county board governs, with a county manager serving as chief administrative officer.
   d. Fairfax County: As Virginia's only designated "urban county," Fairfax operates under powers and procedures specifically tailored for it by the General Assembly. It is governed by a nine-member board of supervisors and a county executive. The two independent cities within Fairfax

County are Falls Church and Fairfax City. They have their own taxing powers and are governed by seven-member councils and city managers but use the county circuit courts. The county's three towns—Vienna, Herndon and Clifton—levy taxes to provide services in addition to those provided by the county, of which they remain a part.

   e. Loudoun County: The county is governed by a seven-member board of supervisors and a county administrator. The county seat is at Leesburg.

   f. Prince William County: A seven-member board of supervisors and a county executive govern the county, whose seat is at Manassas.

E. REGIONAL AGENCIES

   1. Commission of Fine Arts (commonly called the Fine Arts Commission): A federal body that deals with design and esthetics of federal buildings and private buildings in monumental areas, including Pennsylvania Avenue. It also administers the Old Georgetown Act, which restricts permissible design in that neighborhood. (The commission also has limited non-Washington functions, such as approval of the design of military decorations.)

   2. Maryland-National Capital Park and Planning Commission (M-NCPPC): A Maryland state agency that does regional planning for Montgomery and Prince George's counties and maintains parks and a park police force.

   3. Metropolitan Washington Council of Governments (COG): An association of local governments that deals with regional problems and serves as a central research body. It is empowered, among other things, to declare air pollution alerts.

   4. National Capital Parks (NCP): The unit of the

National Park Service that administers the parks and monuments of Washington. It should not be called the National Capital Parks Service.

5. National Capital Planning Commission (NCPC): A federal body that deals with planning, chiefly that which affects the federal government, the District's original L'Enfant plan and federal installations throughout the metropolitan area.

6. Northern Virginia Park Authority (NVPA): An agency that maintains regional (as distinct from local) parks in the area adjacent to D.C. There is also a Fairfax County Park Authority.

7. Northern Virginia Planning District Commission (NVPDC): A state agency established as one of a network of similar bodies statewide to coordinate local planning.

8. Northern Virginia Transportation Commission (NVTC): A Virginia state agency comparable to Maryland's Washington Suburban Transit Commission (see 13). It coordinates the transit policies of Arlington and Fairfax counties and the cities of Alexandria, Falls Church and Fairfax.

9. Transportation Planning Board (TPB): A semiautonomous unit of COG that deals with highways and other transportation matters.

10. Washington Metropolitan Area Transit Authority (WMATA or, preferably, Metro): An interstate authority created by Maryland, Virginia and Congress to construct a rapid rail (partly subway) system and to operate a bus system for the urbanized area. The rail system is called Metrorail; the bus system is called Metrobus.

11. Washington Metropolitan Area Transit Commission (WMATC): An interstate body with the same legal roots as WMATA (Metro). Originally created chiefly

to regulate private transit companies, it now regulates sightseeing services, interstate taxicabs and other similar operations.

12. Washington Suburban Sanitary Commission (WSSC): A Maryland state agency that supplies water and sewerage service to Montgomery and Prince George's counties.

13. Washington Suburban Transit Commission (WSTC): A Maryland state agency that coordinates transit policies of Montgomery and Prince George's counties.

USEFUL REFERENCE BOOKS

Major metropolitan libraries throughout the United States have most of these books on their shelves. Smaller libraries have at least some of them.

A. BIOGRAPHY

Who's Who in America, Who's Who (British) and *Who Was Who in America.* There are *Who's Who* volumes on (among others) Africa, the Arab world, Baltimore, banking, Canada, China, ecology, finance and industry, France, Germany, government, Hollywood, labor, Latin America, Maryland, North American authors, philosophy, politics, science, the screen, show business, steel and metals, the U.S.S.R., Virginia and world Jewry—as well as on America's East, West, Midwest, and South and Southwest.

American Men and Women of Science; the *Biographical Dictionary of American Labor Leaders*; the *Biographical Directory of the American Congress* (including Cabinet lists and members of the Continental Congress); the *Black American Reference Book*; *Burke's Peerage,*

Baronetage & Knighthood; the highly readable *Current Biography*; the classic *Dictionary of American Biography* and its successor, the *Dictionary of National Biography*; the *Dictionary of International Biography*; the *Directory of American Scholars*; the *Blue Book, Green Book, Social Register*, and *Celebrity Register*; the *National Cyclopedia of American Biography*; the *New York Times Obituary Dictionary*.

B. *CONGRESSIONAL DIRECTORY*, which includes:
   1. Lists of all congressional, executive and judicial agencies and their major officials and staff aides, including proper titles and home addresses;
   2. Biographies of all senators and congressmen, their terms, dates of service and committee assignments, and the names of their administrative assistants and secretaries;
   3. Lists of members of congressional committees and names of key committee staff aides;
   4. Lists of state congressional delegations and maps of home districts;
   5. Tables or listings concerning all regular and special sessions of Congress, impeachment actions, state-by-state representation in the House since the first Congress, current governors and their salaries and terms, and all presidents and vice presidents and their terms;
   6. A history of the Capitol and diagrams of it;
   7. Names of U.S. and D.C. courts and biographies of the justices and judges;
   8. Names of high-ranking foreign diplomats in Washington, high-ranking American diplomats abroad and international organizations based there;
   9. A history of the District of Columbia and a list of current officials;

10. Names of individuals and organizations accredited to Senate and House press galleries.

C. DICTIONARIES

The desktop *Webster's New World Dictionary of the American Language* (Collins-World); *Webster's Third New International Dictionary of the English Language* (Merriam); the *Barnhart Dictionary of New English Since 1963*; the *Britannica World Language Edition of Funk and Wagnalls Standard Dictionary* (which emphasizes current spelling and meaning), the exhaustive, multivolume *Oxford English Dictionary* and its recent supplementary volumes; the *Random House Dictionary of the English Language*, *Webster's New Collegiate Dictionary*; the *American Heritage Dictionary of the American Language*; the *International Dictionary in 21 Languages*. For slang, there are: *Eric Partridge's Dictionary of Slang and Unconventional English* (considered the most comprehensive on the subject); Wentworth and Flexner's *Dictionary of American Slang with Supplement* (includes black slang); Anderson's *The Book of Slang.*

D. ENCYCLOPEDIAS

The Encyclopaedia Britannica—15th edition (1974), the 14th edition (1929) and the famous 11th edition (1911); the *Encyclopedia Americana* (strong on science and technology); the one-volume *Columbia Encyclopedia* (especially useful for quickly identifying people and places); *Compton's Picture Encyclopedia*; the *Lincoln Library of Essential Information* (for the elusive fact); the *World Book Encyclopedia* (a favorite with reporters).

E. FEDERAL GOVERNMENT REFERENCES

In addition to the *Congressional Directory*, valuable sources include *Congressional Quarterly* (weekly reports on legislation, presidential actions and federal and state election campaigns); the *Congressional Record* (texts of Senate and House floor discussion and inserted material); *Directory of Registered Lobbyists and Lobbyist Legislation*; the *Government Organization Manual* (descriptions of past and present agencies); the *U.S. Code* (a compilation of federal laws); the *Federal Register, National Journal* and *Presidential Documents* (all dealing with government actions and proposed actions).

F. FOREIGN REFERENCES

Dictionary of Foreign Phrases and Abbreviations; *Keesing's Contemporary Archives* (a weekly looseleaf report on events around the world); *The U.S. Government Printing Office Style Manual* (which lists foreign countries, their capitals, forms of government, moneys and weights and measures, spellings of common words in most major languages and rules for transliteration); *The U.S. State Department Fact Book of the Countries of the World.*

G. GEOGRAPHIC REFERENCES

The Columbia Lippincott Gazetteer of the World; Webster's New World Dictionary.

H. STYLE AND USAGE BOOKS.

A selected bibliography in this field is appended to Chapter V.

INDEX

ABOUT THE AUTHOR

Robert A. Webb worked at The Detroit Free Press as wire
editor, copy desk chief and news editor and has been on The
Washington Post staff since 1965 as day city editor, night
national editor, news editor, picture editor and advisor on
the paper's conversion to an electronic newsroom system.